Listening 2by2: A Paradigm Shift for Leaders
(That's When the Magic Happens!)

By

Tom Kaden and Michael Gingerich

Foreword by Ken Blanchard, co-author of *The One Minute Manager*

Someone To Tell It To
Harrisburg, PA

You make the magic happen!

Published by *Someone To Tell It To, Inc.*
922 N. 3rd Street
Harrisburg, PA 17102
Someone To Tell It To - Contact Us

Quote by Theodore Roosevelt, Theodore Roosevelt - Nobody cares how much you know, until... (brainyquote.com)
Story by David P. Reignhardt, It's Not a Weakness; it's Just Different - Someone To Tell It To

ISBN (Hardcover): 979-8-9850344-2-4
ISBN (Print): 979-8-9850344-0-0
ISBN (eBook): 979-8-9850344-1-7
Library of Congress Control Number: 2021921970

Cover Design by Russ McIntosh
Book Interior Design by VisionIdeaDesign

Printed in the United States of America

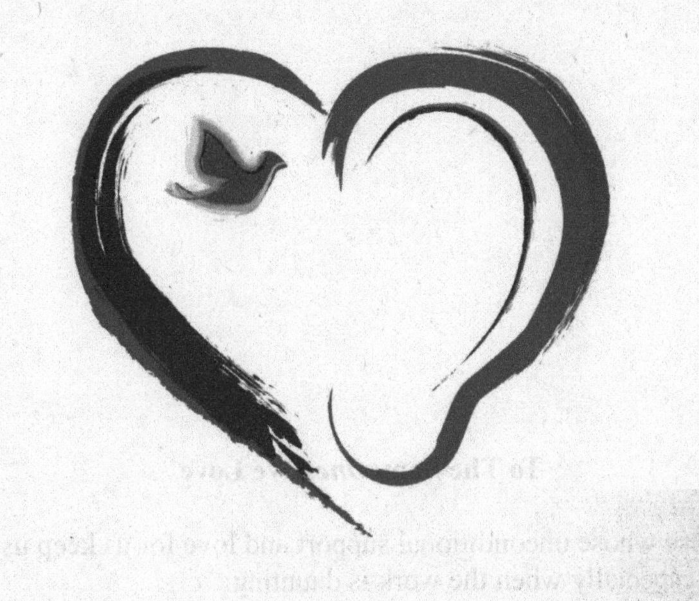

The Symbol

The Listener's symbol

is intended to remind each of us

to take time out of our day

to *see* the faces and *listen* to the voices of

the people we lead,

not only with our ears,

but also, with our hearts.

And to realize that

they are our most important

resources and relationships.

To The Some*Ones* We Love

For those whose unconditional support and love for us keep us going, especially when the work is daunting:

Sarah, Lilly, Luke, Madelyn, and Mya, Kathy, Adam, David, Matthew, Kate, Janelle, Lilyanna, Emma, Emmett, Elle, and Milo.

Your infinite patience, always uplifting presence in our hearts, and constant grace in our imperfections, are overflowing springs of joy and gratitude in our lives. We do this for you, to help create a better world in which you will hear and know that you are valued, vital, and gifts of wonder.

THE PATH TO LISTENING

LISTENING 2BY2 and Someone To Tell It To

It is with great pleasure I write this foreword for *Listening 2by2: A New Paradigm for Leaders* by Tom Kaden and Michael Gingerich. I have known Tom and Michael for several years and have high regard for the vision and mission of *Someone To Tell It To*.

At *Someone To Tell It To,* teams of listeners called *story seekers* are sent out, two by two, to meet with individuals called *story tellers.* Simply put, the story seekers listen while the story tellers talk. For ten years this thoughtful organization has impacted thousands of lives through training in organizations and nonprofits of all sizes. They've built a team of listeners and trainers who encourage and support anyone who has a need to feel heard and to tell their story to someone who will truly listen to them.

Early in their career, most leaders see themselves as good listeners. Over time, however, they become overwhelmed with day-to-day problems that take them away from their best-laid plans for communicating effectively with their people. These leaders may work hard and strive to know every answer and fix every problem—but along the way they've forgotten the value of being a good listener.

Whether you are a leader who serves at home, at work, or elsewhere, listening is an essential leadership skill. And to listen well, you must be *intentional* and *fully present*.

As I told Tom and Michael a few years ago, I wasn't always the best listener. They suggested I was probably a better listener than I thought and reminded me that the first step to becoming an intentional listener is to admit you can improve. It's about consciously making the changes you need to make to become a better listener.

Start with a simple request: "Tell me more." Let the person you are listening to know that their story, their input, and their ideas matter. Everyone has a story to tell that is worth hearing. We all have a need to be heard—and we all can learn to be better at listening.

In this business parable, readers are introduced to a CEO who gets a reminder that he needs to change. Helping him are two listeners who model *Listening 2by2* and help the CEO rediscover his authentic self along the way.

I've often said that the best minute I spend is the one I invest in people. When you invest your time listening to people who live and work around you, you'll experience healthier, happier, more satisfying relationships. Listen to colleagues and team members and create opportunities for collaboration and camaraderie. Listen to family members and unlock lines of communication that may have been shut down. Open your ears and your heart to new people you meet and find value in the smallest interactions.

Great things can happen when you are bold enough to speak your truth and to listen to others speak theirs. When you listen with intention, conversations flourish and take on a life of their own.

Let Tom and Michael show you how to walk on the Path to Listening. It's worth the journey!

Ken Blanchard

Cofounder and Chief Spiritual Officer of The Ken Blanchard Companies®

Coauthor of *The One Minute Manager®* and *Servant Leadership in Action*

ABOUT THE STORY

Experience a paradigm shift through the lens of one person who can transform and affect the culture of his company.

The story I'm about to tell you is for anyone who has ever been in a leadership role as a parent, coach, mentor, teacher, boss, or any other position of influence. It focuses on leaders who are balancing work and home. This story is for anyone who has struggled to motivate others, build trusting relationships, work toward a common goal, or keep employees engaged and passionate about work and their lives.

This is the story of Jeffrey and the time when everything shifted in his life. His journey began on his current path that included working too many hours, having unreasonable expectations of others, failing to appreciate those closest to him, and, not to be forgotten, his struggle to be present with his family, coworkers, and others in his sphere of influence. The path to listening was one of transformation. Jeffrey had to learn how to share responsibilities by developing his ability to listen. Simply listen.

Do you struggle as a leader and believe you must do it all, have the right answers, and be the only decision-maker? Learn, through the example of Vivian and Cecile, the concept of Listening 2by2. Learn to value listening, strength in numbers, story seeking to understand the perspective of others, and the importance facilitating the growth of people at work and within your family.

It's a challenge to leave a positive legacy. Do you recognize when your employees or family members react only when orders are given? Do you feel like the only way things will be accomplished is if you give step-by-step instructions? Or, even more exhausting, you decide to do it yourself because no one else is capable?

What is the truth in all of this? Whose truth is this? Do you *assume* your coworkers and family members *need* the orders, step-by-step instructions, or for you to take over? Are you recognizing that over time they gave up trying to be proactive and creative? Do you recognize that you stopped listening?

In the end, the style of leadership that is commanding and dismissive and the way it functions in an organization is a losing battle for leaders. This style of leadership crushes the soul of the organization (or a home) because people fear contradicting "the boss." Their ideas are rejected, and innovation takes a nosedive.

Jeffrey's story helps you identify a new way of leading by opening your ears to listening, becoming a story seeker, and understanding the strength of Listening 2by2. Experience the paradigm shift through the lens of one person who can transform and affect the culture of his company. Learn to observe people and organizations through a new lens. Realize the value of opening your ears and closing your mouth so you can *actively* and *intentionally* listen to what is being said. Become a story seeker to understand more fully the whole person with whom you are in conversation.

Incorporate Listening 2by2 through which a person has the benefit of attention, guidance, and wisdom from two people at critical moments in their career and life. Using the example of Vivian and Cecile's approach to coaching Jeffrey, you will understand the value of having two distinct listeners offering advice, making observations, and celebrating the transformation of Jeffrey as a leader at work and a partner at home.

Enjoy the story.

ULTIMATUM AND CHOICE

If someone is in a management role,

but isn't a good listener, that person won't

be in a management role for long.

I was at work on a Thursday, anxious to finish the day and go home. Jaime entered my office and stated, "If something doesn't change, I may need to leave the company."

I think this was the first time I truly heard her say something. It was shocking and out of character. Before today, when she spoke I felt like I was hearing the teacher from the Charlie Brown cartoons. White noise, no substance. *Now* she captured my attention. I was listening and heard, loud and clear, her ultimatum.

She was my best manager. Extremely talented and the most likely person to move up in our company. Maybe even take my job. The encounter was an epiphany.

I felt threatened by Jaime. Vulnerability as a manager at its best. Fortunately, I had leverage. You see, I created this beast I call my workplace. I sat at the pinnacle of the organization as the CEO. I ensured systems and processes make the company tick like a finely tuned clock. I made sure someone was in charge. That someone is – ME. It didn't matter that she was, by far, my best employee. Her six years with me have been professional, positive, and productive. I considered myself her mentor. My purpose was to groom her for whatever was next – so long as it wasn't my job.

Jaime's attributes were impressive. Hard worker and loyal, she listened to me and was a perfect sounding board. After we thoroughly discussed ideas, she gave the ideas legs and started the development of each. Her results were impressive. Almost all the projects she managed have been rolled out – concept to implementation – flawlessly and often better than I could have done. She placed the best interests of the organization at the top of her list of priorities every day.

Today she stood in front of my desk with an ultimatum.

My mind raced in search of rhetorical reply. Desperate for what to do, I knew I couldn't lose the person I had come to rely upon. I sat at my desk dumbfounded. My chest tightened and my heart started to race. I was staring at nothing and feeling alone. The silence between us was a deafening scream. "Jaime, can you give me a few minutes. Just fifteen minutes. Can you come back so we can discuss this?"

Her shoulders slumped and she shook her head in disbelief. "Sure." She turned and practically stomped out of the room. If I had had the right kind of door to my office, I'm sure she would have slammed it.

I took a deep breath and rested my head in the palm of my hands. I thought this would stop the pounding at my temples and the ringing in my ears. Finally, I recalled two women who were presenters at a TEDx event I attended at the local university. They were introduced as the *Listeners* and credited with developing a new leadership theory and practice known as Listening 2by2. They earned their notoriety by helping managers become keenly aware of an often-overlooked key to communication - listening. Incorporating listening into the business's DNA has led to paradigm shifts and culture change. Organizations have moved from communicating in silos, to one of inclusion, open communication, and respect.

I remember how the Listeners spoke of their *great awakening*. They described having to look in the mirror after a particularly difficult conversation with an employee - *one of their stars*. They had been blindsided by this trusted member of their inner circle when he threatened to quit. He declared, quite painfully for the Listeners, that there were others on the team who were thinking about the same thing. They realized that something had to change. As deflating as it was to admit, that *something* was really *someone*. They had to change.

I couldn't believe I found myself in the same situation. I yanked open the top drawer of my desk fully prepared to dig for their card. There it was like a beacon on top of my box of paper clips. Within five minutes of calling, I had an appointment to meet with them the next day.

When Jaime returned to my office I asked her *why*. She told me her reasons and all I could do was stare and listen. I tried defending myself several times, but she was ready. I felt anger welling up and wanted to lash out. She must have sensed what was coming because she abruptly stood up and suggested we continue this conversation the next day. "You'll have some time to consider what I've brought to you." She turned and not only left me at my desk but also left for the day – an hour early. My meeting with the Listeners couldn't come soon enough.

MEETING MY LISTENERS: VIVIAN AND CECILE

To become a listener, it is essential to first believe that everyone matters and is significant.

Our appointment was for 8 a.m. I walked into the trendy coffee shop that sold only fair-trade coffee and had walls covered with the art of local artists. I'm positive French music softly played in the background barely audible through the sounds of ceramic coffee cups, morning conversations, and names announced when an order was ready.

I recognized them immediately. They were sitting on one of the worn-out sofas that looked like it had been rescued from sure death at a landfill. I was surprised at my reaction because I loved it!

The first woman sat in utter comfort; arms stretched across the back of the sofa claiming her territory. She was wearing casual clothes, earrings that brushed her shoulders and short hair that accentuated her youthful features. I chuckled imagining her in the 1970s wearing bell bottom jeans, a psychedelic shirt, and a hairstyle that reflected the rebellious disposition of so many of that era.

Next to her sat her business partner. Petite, about 60 years old with silver blond hair cut in a bob, and pink lipstick that had to be intentionally bright. She was also dressed casually but with a flair that I could only consider "proper." Her posture was that of a ballerina who no longer danced but remembers how to execute every move. I guess I have listened to my wife and daughters more than I thought. I didn't realize how in tune I could be to the details of how women dress and look.

They were deep in conversation, laughing and leaning in toward each other so they could hear. Somehow they recognized me. I don't know how but the smiles were captivating, and they waved me over in unison. I indicated I would order my coffee first and be there shortly.

Each rose as I approached and shook my hand covering it with their free hand. I sat down in a red-velvet Queen Anne-style armchair that sagged a little too low under my weight. Maybe I was in need of my own *great awakening* too – about my weight. I thanked them profusely for the meeting acknowledging their busy schedules. "What I'd like to discuss won't take much of your time."

"Don't be silly. We have plenty of time. It's our pleasure to meet with you. How about we start with introductions?" Her husky voice was reassuring and informal. I noted a subtle southern accent masked by the influence of the northeast. "I know you know of us as the Listeners but it's probably better to be on a first-name basis, don't you think? My name is Vivian. This is Cecile," she patted her friend's hand lovingly. "We'll be meeting with you if you want to continue after today."

Happy to hear there could be more meetings, I gushed, "I was astonished when I first heard you talk about listening in pairs. Could you remind me of the reasons behind it?"

"Absolutely. It's how our business operates. Our team of listeners always arrive in pairs. Listening 2by2, we call it. We believe four ears are better than two. Two hearts are bigger than one. We want to be sure you know we're listening. Now, we're interested to hear your story. What would you like to discuss, honey? There's nothing you can't say to us. We're all ears." With that, she leaned in.

I must admit hearing someone call me *honey* made me a little uncomfortable. I wasn't sure what to say and decided to let it go. Then Cecile smiled and chuckled. She must have seen something in my reaction to being called *honey*. Even with that, I felt their presence was comforting, and I knew I had made the right decision to call.

Our drinks arrived, chamomile tea for Cecile, double espressos for Vivian and me. "Gotta love a man who likes his coffee strong," Vivian toasted me and Cecile before sipping her robust brew.

Then it was my turn and I let it flow. I told them what happened the day before, about my follow up with Jaime, and the anxiety I experienced ever since. I confessed, "I can't understand why she is threatening to quit. After all, I've always paid her well! I thought we had a good working relationship. I guess not. What I'm dealing with goes beyond my work-related issues."

I finished my coffee and continued. What I said next was possibly the most vulnerable thing I had ever told anyone.

"Even more importantly, my wife told me she needs some space. What exactly does that mean?" I held in the tears that were burning on the rims of my eyes. Men don't cry, I reminded myself.

Vivian and Cecile did what they do best - they listened, paid attention, and heard the things I was saying out loud. They seem to hear what I left unsaid, hidden in my heart. Their interest in me seemed genuine. I couldn't believe what I was saying. I revealed an aspect of myself I never share. Today I shared it with two complete strangers.

After a lengthy pause, Vivian responded with the most empathetic words I needed in that fragile moment when my career and life were topsy-turvy.

"I'm so sorry. Thank you for being vulnerable and your desire to find a new way to live. A new way to communicate and be in this world." I felt my shoulder drop and my spine gave way to the heavy burden I was carrying.

She let me soak in the moment then continued, "May I share a little bit of wisdom I learned in the good 'ole school of hard knocks?"

"Sure. Please," I remembered to include. I glanced at Cecile who was watching my every move and listening to every word. "That's why I'm here."

"When was the last time you simply listened to Jaime and those closest to you?"

"What do you mean? She's in and out of my office all the time. We work very closely together. I hear every word she says."

"We hear birds singing, horns honking, and dishes being stacked while we sit here. Hearing is passive. Let me clarify. I didn't say *just* listen, Jeffrey. I said, *simply* listen. There's a difference. Let me explain.

"Bartenders have claimed that although customers pay for their drinks, what they are really paying for is someone to *simply listen* to them. A bartender confided in me that lonely people don't come to a bar just to drink. They can drink at home and a lot cheaper. They go to the bar to find someone who will *simply listen* to them. Bartenders fill that role."

I looked a little puzzled, still not understanding what she meant. I considered myself a good listener. It was Cecile's turn.

"Let me try to explain," her British accent was thick. "There are no 10-step shortcuts to listen better. Listening is not meant to be checked off a to-do list. There is no magic formula and *poof!* you're a world-class listener. Listening is not merely something you do. It is informed by what you believe about other people. Insincerity is not masked by nodding your head and saying *uh-huh,* so you appear to be listening. People know when you are not paying attention and being disingenuous.

"To become a listener, it is essential to first *believe* that everyone matters and is significant. You must believe to your core the essence of human needs includes being heard through active listening. It is essential to believe that being heard will make a profound difference for people to gain a sense of dignity and self-worth and, eventually, passion for their jobs. If they know they are heard, respected for their insights, and valued as a member of the team, they will care more and become more engaged."

"That isn't limited to the workplace. It includes your family," chimed Vivian.

Cecile leaned in further, her face no more than two inches in front of mine. Vivian sat back on the couch and smiled. Everything and everyone in the coffee shop disappeared. Though Cecile was actively engaged, both were completely focused on me. I could smell the chamomile tea and the sweetness of the honey she added.

"A person who does not believe in the dignity and worth of others will not truly listen. People pick up on that. They often perceive that they are not being heard and feel devalued. It affects their performance. It causes them to give less of themselves. This leads to a manager's, and other leaders, inability to ask for, let alone demand, the best from their employees. Leaders understand the need for humans to be valued for their role in any organization. Without trust and sincerity, organizations cannot thrive."

I was beginning to feel uncomfortable and started fidgeting in my seat. No longer locking eyes with either listener who sat with me, I was suddenly conscious of the other people in the room who were staring at us. Vivian never missed a beat.

"Jeffrey," Vivian smoothly reengaged, "don't worry. What Cecile just shared is a lot to absorb. We've both been there. It's one of the reasons why we've been friends for 30 years and started our business. Our goal is to create an inclusive world where everyone feels valued.

"There are a lot of people who may say everyone has value and significance - and they may believe it - but they fail to simply listen. Listening is constant, purposeful, and a lifelong process.

None of us listens perfectly. That's why our teams always go out in twos. We have to consciously make the choice to listen on a daily basis. Having a partner who's also engaged and listening ensures that the fullest amount of the story someone is sharing is heard. We seek out the stories others *want to*, and sometimes *must*, share. We are story seekers who listen with intention."

"It's what you believe?" I whispered.

Cecile winked and smiled at her old friend. Vivian couldn't hide her enthusiasm as she sat back on the tattered sofa. She crossed her blue jean clad legs and picked up her coffee. They had listened intently to all I had to share. I was beginning to understand the purpose behind listening. Did I value it? I couldn't honestly say.

We stood on the sidewalk where I tried to continue the conversation. Then Vivian asked me, "Have you ever heard of the philosophers Epictetus and Plato?" I shook my head. "Epictetus once stated that *We have two ears and one mouth so that we can listen twice as much as we speak.* On par with that sentiment, Plato suggested *Wise men speak because they have something to say; Fools because they have to say something.*

"Before we go our separate ways, I have another question for you to think about before our next meeting."

I listened with anticipation for our second meeting and felt the relief when she made that declaration.

"Think of the leaders in your life – parents, mentors, coaches, friends, and managers - who listened to you. Then answer this: What made each a good listener?"

I stood before the two of them wanting to answer right away but realized that I should take the time to think this through. I recognized that I had taken enough of their valuable time.

They smiled and asked if it would be okay to give me a hug. Grateful for their gracious demeanor and sincerity, I allowed myself to be embraced by both. We agreed to meet again at the same time and location the following week.

I watched as the best friends turned and hooked their arms while they strolled like two schoolgirls down the sidewalk. Neither had a concern in the world. I wanted to hear more about believing in others, but they made it clear it was time to leave. "We have to go. Our families are expecting us."

I had just taken the first step on the path to listening.

REFLECTING ON MY ENCOUNTERS

You need to be heard and valued as much

as anyone else needs to be heard and valued.

No one promised this would be easy.

I turned to walk back to my office. My head was swirling from my first meeting with Vivian and Cecile, my listeners, and memories of the moment when Jaime entered my office. Her ultimatum and my conversations with my wife were pivot points that would forever change my future.

For six years, Jaime gave so much to the company. Her work ethic was impeccable. She is always unfailingly polite, respected by co-workers, kind, and pleasant to work with. Reliably engaging with the members of her team, she doesn't ask them to do anything she wouldn't do or hasn't already done. A model employee with potential to advance and maybe sprint past me.

Even after meeting with Vivian and Cecile, I still felt a tinge of anger and jealousy. What did I learn from my first encounter with them? Their body language was open and engaging. They made eye contact. Cecile leaned in removing any barriers between us and distractions within the coffee shop. I felt a little overwhelmed by that alone. Can I do that? Can I be open and welcoming? Can I smile and laugh more often?

As soon as I returned to my office, I tried it out with my assistant. "Good morning, Melody. How are you today?" I intentionally stopped in front of her desk, leaned over, and looked her straight in the eyes. The look on her face validated how I was feeling. Awkward and uncomfortable.

"Mr. Stone are you okay?," she asked leaning back in her chair putting more distance between us.

I took a deep breath, "I'm great. Just want to be sure you are too." I was hoping my smile looked relaxed because my face felt stiff.

Then, a subtle smile appeared, "I'm fantastic! Went on a great run this morning. Training for my marathon, remember?"

Keep smiling, keep smiling I warned myself. I didn't recall her telling me she was training for a marathon. "That's great. How far was the run?"

"Sixteen miles. All flat, thankfully. I went to one of the rails-to-trails parks. You should try it."

"I should, you're right," I chuckled as I stood up and patted my loose stomach.

"Please hold my calls until 11 this morning." I remembered to say please with a smile.

"Of course, Mr. Stone. Thanks for asking how my morning is going," she swung in her chair and bounced to the copier.

I turned and practically ran to my office closing the door behind me. Uncomfortable. Completely uncomfortable. I prayed she didn't think I was being a creep. I needed a few hours to think about my meeting with the listeners, Jaime's ultimatum, and about what I just did. I let myself be vulnerable and… nice. I attempted to let a barrier down and be genuinely interested. "I won't forget about the marathon training," I whispered aloud as I wrote myself a note.

I also had to prepare for another meeting with Jaime. So many people told me about the notes they received from Jaime. Apparently she wrote scores of thank you and congratulatory notes, celebrating her team as individuals, not simply what they produced for the company. She made it a point to engage and get to know each person she managed. She knew what each employee valued because she listened.

When Sandy needed quality time - due to her husband's recent passing, her loneliness was palpable - Jaime took her to a favorite restaurant for lunch. She was intentionally present when Sandy shared stories about her husband's life as well as the personal demands his unexpected passing placed on her. Was Jaime a story seeker?

If John valued results, she stopped by his office to thank him every time a project was completed on time. If Saeed needed help on a given project, she would meet with him one-on-one until he felt confident in the outcome. If Shanta had a stressful week, both at home and at work, Jaime would bring her fresh vegetables from her garden, knowing Shanta was on a strict diet due to some recent health complications.

Her team never had a negative comment to say. They loved and respected her and offered support in her times of need.

I felt the heat rise on my neck as I considered all of this. Jealousy and resentment started to fill my thoughts. Then insecurity settled in. How could I change? Did I want to be like Jaime?

How well did I know my employees? For that matter, how well did I know my family?! What did I believe about other people? I sat in my office, undisturbed, for two hours making notes on everyone I could think of who worked for me and then started a second notebook for my family. I had a game plan for the rest of the day. Lean in, remove the barriers, look people in the eye, ask questions and – listen. *Two ears and one mouth.* I felt confident and then Jaime knocked on my door.

ULTIMATUM, ROUND TWO

Why is it that some managers seem to develop a positive work culture, where everyone is trusted, respected, and valued, and others don't?

"Yep, come on in." She stepped inside, smiling as usual, and my plan went down the tube.

"Have a seat," I pointed to the chair in front of my desk, my voice terse. I made myself comfortable in my new ergonomically designed executive chair. I was back in charge!

As she sat down, envy coursed through my veins. Thinking back, I realized how much she listens. Simply listens. Her employees are a priority, and she models the characteristics of a leader I wished I could emulate. She doesn't care about being credited for the company's success, even though everyone else at the office knows she's the mover and shaker. She simply wants to do excellent work, inspire her team members to do their very best, and create a working environment that produces great results. All along the way, every day, having a good time.

The pit of my stomach tightened.

2by2 crossed my mind. *Could I partner with Jaime? Could I partner with my wife?* Discomfort forced me to adjust my position in my ergonomically now incorrect and uncomfortable chair.

As much as I wanted to dislike her, I didn't. I valued the work but maybe not the person who sat on the other side of my desk every day. I shook my head.

"Is everything okay?"

"Sure, why?"

"You're shaking your head and your face looks like you just found out something terrible."

I didn't realize my body language was speaking my thoughts. I intentionally shook my head, breathed in deeply, and let out a long breathe. "I'm good. Just have some things on my mind."

I looked at the desk between us and thought I should move to the chair next to her. Did I have the courage? I shook my head again, took a deep breath, and got up. When I sat down the look on her face spoke volumes about who I had become. She shifted uncomfortably in her seat.

In that moment I realized how a desk served as a barrier. It was also a distraction. My office was not conducive to meaningful communication. I had to remove my mental barrier to step from behind the physical barrier. For Jamie, removing barriers was second nature.

Our conversation lasted an hour and I returned to my desk after she left the office. I felt good about what we discussed. I practiced leaning in, removing barriers, and intentionally listened. I took notes, asked questions, and spoke only when I needed to. I thought it was great!

That afternoon, the tension in the office was reaching a boiling point. I don't know why I didn't see this coming. Old feelings started to surface, and I perceived Jaime was intentionally outshining me. In my more rational moments, I knew that wasn't the case. I was the boss, right?

Boss, huh? Jaime is my greatest asset. Why am I anxious and intimidated? We just had a great talk. Greatest asset... I probably rarely made her feel as if she were. I had a duel going on inside my mind. Anger and Jealousy vs Openness and Appreciation. Which would win, I had no clue.

I now knew the mountain I needed to climb and the nemesis I had to defeat – my own way of being and, frankly, Jaime. It wasn't really Jaime but my perception of her and my assumption that I needed to be more like her instead of finding my authentic self.

Rarely, if ever, did I spend time getting to know *Jaime's* thoughts, desires, hopes, dreams, fears, and joys. Rarely, if ever, did I send a hand-written note thanking her for a job well done. Rarely, if ever, had I acknowledged the late nights at the office, despite the fact that Jaime had three small children at home. That wasn't fair. That wasn't being a leader.

I had made my relationship with her a transactional one, only seeming to care about what she could produce, no matter the cost to her well-being or sense of worth. I was neglecting her as a human being, a person with feelings and a need to be appreciated and respected. I began to realize that I was making her feel as if she was neither valuable as a professional nor as a person. In a nutshell, I lacked compassion.

Like I said, my plans from the morning went out the window. Even with the conversation Jaime and I had earlier in my office, by that afternoon, *Anger* and *Jealousy* won the battle in my mind and the old me came barreling back.

Here's how our afternoon conversation transpired.

"Jaime, I'd like you to come to my office. Please sit down." I shut the door and assumed my seat behind the desk. In my hand was a legal pad overflowing with my thoughts.

"Let me start with this. I consider you an asset to our company. However, I have some concerns."

I then proceeded to read from a list of more than a dozen observations of what she had done wrong and that I felt were undermining my authority.

"Everyone in the company keeps going to you every time something positive happens. You always get the credit. Why is that? I'm the leader of this company, yet you seem to forget that!"

The look on her face should have told me to stop. It was a mix between anger, despair, and defeat. I feared I had pushed her over the edge, and she would quit on the spot. *What are you doing?* I scolded myself. But I couldn't stop. She didn't get a word in. As usual, she listened.

There was something else bothering me that day. I realized I was more easily irritated over the previous six months. I couldn't understand what it was until that moment while I continued my tirade. It all bubbled to the surface.

I was a jerk – at home and at work. I didn't laugh like I used to, and I didn't speak to anyone. Since becoming CEO, my perspective on life and perception of who I should be changed.

After the meeting concluded, Jaime, with tears rolling down her face, quickly rushed to the women's room to regain her composure. I followed her to the door of my office with pride and a new feeling – embarrassment. I glanced at my assistant who looked terrified as she watched Jaime enter the ladies' room.

My timing was unfortunate. Still to be accomplished was a presentation in the afternoon about a book Jaime had published six weeks prior. I couldn't hide my envy. It was about positive workplaces and creating a caring, supportive culture. I had just given her a perfect case study for the absence of all three. I was tone deaf. Heartless. Insensitive. My heart sank to the pit of my stomach. I sabotaged her big moment. Was it intentional? I was perpetuating and exemplifying anything but a caring culture. I was doing damage that was going to take a long time and a lot of work to overcome.

Jaime had made connections after publishing the book and it's why she was considering leaving. I didn't understand how she did it. I hadn't made connections. What did that mean? I couldn't and wouldn't celebrate her success because I didn't understand and never listened to her as she went through the process of writing it. As I considered this, I realized I missed an opportunity to connect, understand, and listen. Melody's marathon training was another perfect example of my tone deafness.

A moment later, Jaime came back into my office and declared for the second time that if things didn't change, she will leave the company. The operative word in this instance was "will." I had never seen her so frustrated, so blunt. I know now it was manifested frustration born of hurt. And I was the perpetrator.

There it was - *my* moment, *my* opportunity to connect with Jaime and grasp her perspective. Finally, I realized something, or better yet *someone*, needed to change. That someone was me. The something was my attitude. I realized I took my title as CEO from the perspective of transactional management. I didn't understand what it meant to lead.

My way of looking at and interacting with others whom I not only managed but also had to lead was affecting the culture of the organization. To recognize opportunities to build relationships, I needed to start in my own mind and heart. First, I had to take a good hard look at what I was doing (or not doing) at home. Changes there would carry over to work. I had a chance to reinvent myself and develop a solid, collaborative relationship with my wife and children and, by extension, Jaime and others who work as part of our team. *Our team. That sounds nice. Not my team. Our team.*

I closed my office door more out of embarrassment than for privacy. I checked my calendar and noticed Melody had not put my meeting with Vivian and Cecile on it. I sent her an email asking her to be sure to add it. I couldn't muster the courage to open my door and ask her face-to-face. The look of horror she had when Jaime left my office earlier shook me to my core. When I refreshed my calendar, there it was. I sent her a thank you.

That appointment couldn't come soon enough. 2by2 they would arrive to be sure they would hear my full story by listening with intention.

THE FIRST STROKE TO CLEAR THE PATH

"Nobody cares how much you know

until they know how much you care."

Theodore Roosevelt

The following week I entered the progressive, hippy-throwback coffee shop. Vivian and Cecile were sitting in the corner next to the window listening to another person. When she saw me, Vivian put up one finger to ask for a little more time so they could finish. I nodded and went to the counter to order my double espresso. When the barista asked me what I would like, I took a chance. "Hi! How are you today?" I looked right at her and leaned in.

She smiled broadly, glowing with sunshine. "Great! It's been a little busy, but I like it that way. Helps the time go by. Besides, I have an exam tomorrow that I'm really nervous about. What'll you take?"

I almost ordered the double espresso. "Tea. Mint tea." I was shocked to hear that come out of my mouth.

"Wow! Last week you ordered a double shot espresso. Big change. What size?"

Hold on. She remembered *me*?! Last week was the first time I had ever stepped into this place. Honestly, I thought it was full of unsavory people. I don't remember seeing her or even hearing her ask me for my order. I was probably too busy looking around or down at the counter. "Thanks for remembering me. Yep, trying to do things a little differently. I'm sorry I don't remember you. What's the exam?"

"Chemistry. I'm a pre-med major."

Oh my gosh! Tattoos. A pierced nose. And more earrings attached to her ears than I can count on two hands. She is studying to become a doctor?! "Good golly! Seriously?," rushed out of my mouth before I could stop myself.

She had a full-throated laugh. "I get that all the time. I love to see people's reactions. Yep. I've wanted to be a doctor since I was about ten. My little brother was diagnosed with leukemia. That'll be three seventy-five."

I looked for a name tag so I could put the name with the face. I had to remember this girl. "Luca. I hope you ace your exam."

"Thanks! Me too."

I stepped aside to wait for my tea. Vivian and Cecile were deep in conversation. The lady who was with them had left. I turned to smile and wave to let them know I would be there soon. In the most elegant way I had ever seen, Cecile reassured me she wasn't going anywhere. It looked like she had lessons in etiquette from the Queen of England.

Something was different about Vivian who stared at me with twinkling eyes. Her hair? She wore all white today. Linen? Why was I so concerned about the details? I'm never concerned about the details of another person. They waived me over and I grinned like a second grader who was being acknowledged by his teacher.

They both stood and we exchanged a bro-hug – handshake and shoulder tap half -hug with a pat on the back. I felt reassured they were very happy to see me and ready to hear my story. The tension in my shoulders began to release.

Luca brought my tea and I looked directly at her to say thank you when I took the cup.

"I was watching you," Vivian declared. "Something has changed. You made Luca smile and she rarely smiles. Serious pre-med student and all. She's focused."

"I have been trying to do things a little differently. I noticed last week how Cecile leaned in and made me feel like I was the only one in the coffee shop. You simply listened," I couldn't help but use the phrase.

"I've been trying to do that all week, but it hasn't been easy."

"You didn't become a non-listener overnight and you won't become a listener even in a week. It takes commitment and is an intentional practice."

I nodded. I was thinking about Jaime and my encounters with her – the good and the unfortunate. And about my attempt to be intentional at home and with Melody and her marathon training. Then there's the list of past leaders I put together to share what made them good listeners. I filled them in on the past week and how I felt uncomfortable, inauthentic, not like myself and had some introspective breakthroughs. The two of them simply listened. "I have my list. It's not long," I remarked. "But I do think it describes some of what those individuals exemplified when they listened well to me. I even included Jaime and the way she interacts with me and other team members. Here goes nothin'."

1. They pay attention and focus on my needs.
2. They care about what I have to say.
3. Even though they may be busy, they make time for me.
4. They don't interrupt me, tell me what to do or what to believe.
5. They don't give their opinion unless I ask for it.
6. They ask probing questions.
7. They keep checking in on me and want to know more.

"That's an excellent list and it's *something*," Vivian reassured me. "Tell us what you learned."

"Well," I hesitated. "This is hard to admit, but there are two people currently in my life who exemplify those characteristics. My wife, Amanda, and… Jaime."

Taking a deep breath, I poured out why I was frustrated. My jealousy and envy were obvious. "I am a hard worker. I try to treat my employees with respect. I *do* listen when they speak. At least I thought I was listening until I tried to incorporate some of what you demonstrated last week and reviewed the list of what good listeners in my life have done."

Cecile took a sip of tea and Vivian sat back knowing she had words of wisdom to share. Neither jumped in to scorn me. Neither shook their heads as if to tell me what a fool I am and acknowledge my mistakes. Nothing judgmental. All they did was sit in silence with me until I was finished. Then Cecile was ready.

"Someone once gave me an acronym to use as a reminder of why intentional communication is important to human interaction. Part of communicating, and maybe the most important act of communication, is the ability to receive what someone is saying and absorb its significance. The acronym is L-I-S-T-E-N. *Listen.*"

"Go figure," Vivian added with a chuckle.

"I have a note card that has been on my desk for years. It's literally been a game-changer personally and professionally. I brought a copy with me today."

She handed me the card. It read:

<u>LISTEN</u>

***L**ean In and Remove Barriers*

***I**nterested and Curious*

***S**implify and Self-Care*

***T**alk Less and Embrace Silence*

***E**xplain and Ask Questions*

***N**egotiate the Win-Win*

I read trying to absorb its significance. "That is an easy way to remember. Could you help me understand each attribute? I mean, as I think about it a moment, I've experienced things on the list from those who have listened well to me. But I need help in re-shaping who I am, how I am, and my leadership style. To find my authentic self as a listener. I know how to manage systems and processes. It's my leadership style that obviously hasn't been achieving the kind of results I long for in my relationships at home and at work. I say this humbly, and that's not easy. I have a lot to learn from leaders who listen. This is difficult to admit but Jaime is one of those leaders I can learn from as well as the two of you."

"And you and Amanda, your wife," Vivian declared with a wink and a laugh. "The two of you are leaders too. Maybe you just need a little refining and reflection on the times you have been the leader you believe you should be."

"It's a process of discovery and rediscovery," Cecile added. "We all have the characteristics of the people we wish we could be. It's a matter of being reminded and overcoming the habits, obstacles, and mindsets that have kept us from evolving."

I felt the blood rushing to my face. It was weird to have someone my mother's age wink at me. I felt like I was ten years old. It was kind of nice. I suppose we all want someone to speak to the child that has always existed and needs to be recognized on occasion.

"We're happy to explain each of them," she continued. "Remember, you are not alone. I had to learn these very same principles too. In fact, I wish I had learned them much, much sooner. The person who helped me through this metamorphosis is now my business partner.

"My hope as I transformed was that I did not find that I hurt people I care about, trust, appreciate, value, and love. If I had, I prayed they would forgive me. Through this process, maybe I, too, would achieve even greater results. And I have."

Cecile continued. It was evident she was the storyteller. "I'm reminded of a seminar I attended several years ago in which the speaker was the author David P. Reinhardt. He spoke about his deep love for Alaskan husky dogs and his participation in the annual Iditarod.

"There was a point Reinhardt made during his presentation that resonated strongly with me. He started describing each of the huskies on his team and what his dogs have taught him about life and leadership. He spoke about the dogs by name and listed the special attributes of each — one's energy, another's patience, another's stamina, and another's sense of direction. He also listed each of their unique characteristics — being easily distracted, aloofness, skittish, or a slower gait.

"When Reinhardt described each husky, he didn't discuss their strengths and then say, *But here are his weaknesses, here are her flaws*. Instead, he said, *These are her strengths,* or *These are other aspects of his personality*. It was subtle but he spoke volumes with his choice of words. Reinhardt wasn't saying that the dogs had no weaknesses. He was saying instead that they simply had unique and different characteristics from one another. He was saying that each was unequaled, that each offered distinctive attributes that *added something valuable* to the team. He was saying that each had gifts that were important and that mattered.

"His message served as a valuable reminder to me about the point I continually reinforce - we all matter. A dog sled team can't run a successful race without the unique contributions of the entire team. Neither can a successful organization fulfill its mission without the unique contributions of all its members. We must believe in and embrace the special and wonderful attributes of everyone on the team. It starts with believing that everyone has value and something vital to offer. This fundamental belief is the foundation to intentional, active listening. Start with the belief, Jeffrey, that everyone has something valuable to teach us. That everyone has a story to tell. Become a story seeker."

I took a deep breath and tried to avert my eyes but the cool blueness of hers would not allow me to look away.

"Listening starts here," she pointed to her heart.

"I never thought of it that way. I always thought it was about eye contact, parroting what others are saying, not interrupting - things like that. I never thought about first shifting what I fundamentally believe about people, seeking their stories, or that everyone needs to be listened to. You're giving me a lot to think about."

Vivian spoke up to drive home the point – her role in today's conversation. "I'm glad you're beginning to think about listening in a new way, Jeffrey. It'll help you become the listener who already exists inside of you and a better human being. You'll see your leadership style change and evolve and communication at home will improve and strengthen. Priorities will change – for the better. We're restoring our communities when we listen with intention."

I was anxious to start. I tried to dive into discussing the "L" of the acronym.

"Hold on, my brother," Vivian put her hand up. "Priorities. Remember, priorities. We'll start today with ours - family. They are waiting for us. But before we go, I want to point out that you have already been practicing "L" – lean in and remove barriers. Think about what you have shared with us. Your actions over the last week. One more thing. If you're not uncomfortable, you're not growing, you're not evolving, you're not moving through a transformative process. Get comfortable with being uncomfortable. We'll start next week."

We said good-bye after agreeing to meet again the following week. With my permission, they both gave me the hugs my mother used to give me and which I realized I missed and hadn't given my children in a long time.

I watched them hook arms again, laugh, and glide, in step with each other, out of the coffee shop. I purposefully stayed behind to say good-bye to Luca and wish her good luck on the exam. "I'll be back next week. I'll expect to hear all about it," I smiled and turned to leave.

I still had a few more things to do at the office. As I walked back, I was thinking about the last thing Vivian said about priorities. I pulled out my cell phone, called Melody and told her I was done for the day, and she should go home too, "You need to recover from your training run so you can finish the marathon." The voice on the other end of the call was elated and shocked. She thanked me profusely and assured me the meetings I had on my schedule were not important and she would reschedule all of them before she left the office.

Cecile's voice echoed in my head as I walked to the parking lot. "If you focus on developing an organization's culture - treating others as you would like to be treated - it will make a positive difference. If you ask those you lead how they'd like to be treated, and then intentionally listen to their answers and respectfully consider them, you will have the beginning of a transformed culture that helps people be excited and enthusiastic about their work. That results in better service, better products, and success. The same is true with your family. I recommend you start there. It will carry over to work."

With new-found energy and a desire in my heart to be with my wife and daughters that I had not felt in years, I put my car in gear and left for home – music blaring through the speakers. Another long-forgotten love of mine, music.

I was fascinated by the LISTEN acronym, believing in the value of others, seeking their stories, and being open to learn from others. That last point was a challenge since I felt I had to have all the answers all the time. I had to admit it was a relief to feel like I didn't have to be *that* person, the one who was firing all cylinders and always in charge. Leadership is about developing others, understanding their strengths and weaknesses. Finding the right combination of team members who complement each other. The best way I can do that is to listen.

The key to transformation and culture shifts, I was learning, is to understand that we reinforce best practices by taking what we learn, implementing plans, learning from the activity, evaluating, adapting, and continuing the loop. I had a plan for the next week. It would start with sitting down with Melody to revamp my calendar. And, even more important, I had to be sure to ask about her marathon training and intentionally listen.

"L"
LEAN IN AND REMOVE BARRIERS

Listening is an art, as well as a science. It's not merely what you do, but it's what you know and believe about other people.

It was pouring down rain about fifteen minutes before my next meeting with Vivian and Cecile. I thought about rescheduling then decided a little rain wouldn't hurt me. I grabbed the largest umbrella I could find and left for the coffee shop.

I arrived about five minutes late and there they sat, bone dry, at the corner table. I saw two brightly colored umbrellas leaning against the wall, one with a puddle of water at its base. They looked refreshed and ready to go. *How do they always look so calm?* They waved me over. On the table were three cups and a tea pot.

"I ordered for all of us. I assumed you wouldn't mind," Cecile's British accent made everything seem perfect and proper.

I shrugged off my coat and tried not to get either of them wet. "Thank you. Sorry I'm a little late. I thought about calling to reschedule, the rain and all."

"I'm always prepared," Vivian declared with a sly smile as she peered at me over her teacup. "Unless I'm sick in bed, I make my appointments. Usually arrive early and today was a perfect day for that. The rain started when I was about half a block from the shop. I got lucky. Cecile was already here. She always beats me to our appointments." Vivian smiled at her best friend and then nodded her head toward my drenched shoes and pants. They laughed so hard I thought everyone would stop what they were doing just to try to find out what was so funny.

I knew the humor was at my expense, but I laughed too, a little harder than I intended but I was feeling true joy. The past week had been great.

"Let's dive right in," Vivian managed to puff out between giggles. "I'll start. This isn't how we usually do this, but we agreed you probably need to hear this." I leaned in and a sly smile appeared at the corners of her mouth.

"You are already way ahead of a lot of people who think they are good listeners. People's appraisal of their listening skill is much like their assessment of their driving skill or their leadership. The bulk of adults think they're above average. They're not. As a result, too many adults stop paying attention. They stop growing."

Vivian opened a binder lying next to her and pulled out an envelope. "I call this my affirmation envelope. Throughout my career, I've kept every encouraging note I've ever received to remind me of the times I led well and effectively and truly made a difference for someone."

"What a great idea! I wouldn't need a large envelope. I've never received affirmations - written or spoken," I confessed, sadly.

She continued after giving me a knowing glance. "You won't receive if you don't give, Jeffrey. It helps me to keep practicing what I preach about good listening, good leadership, and good management. Let me read my most recent affirmation."

She pulled it out and gently unfolded the letter as though it were a fragile gift. "On one of my social media accounts I shared: *When you walk into someone else's life, leave it brighter than you found it. Give generously. Smile abundantly. Listen diligently.*

"One of my managers sent me a private message:

I hope I did this enough today thanks to your leadership... Will try again tomorrow, and again the next day, thank you for the gentle reminder.

"Her response is the one I seek. It's about learning, growing, implementing, and changing what needs to change, day after day after day. Can I ask you to make a commitment with us today, Jeffrey? Will you commit to meeting once a week for an hour to talk through each one of the six LISTEN principles?"

"Really? I thought we were going to go over all of them today. You'd do that with me? Meet six times? Well, today plus five more weeks?"

"Absolutely! We'd be glad to. We have learned to simplify our schedules, one of the principles of the LISTEN acronym, to prioritize time to listen. It's that important to us."

Without hesitation I responded, "I'm in! I know I need to change. If I don't my family may suffer, and Jaime may leave. If she leaves, I may be done too."

"Then let's get started. First principle is ***L*** *– Lean In and Remove Barriers*. Literally, physically lean in closer to the person you're listening to. When you do, you're saying to the other person, *In this moment, you are the most important person in my life*. Removing mental barriers is more of a challenge. But if you practice the principles, your way of thinking will change too.

"As you've already been experiencing, you'll become more observant and sensitive to the environment. You'll begin to understand better and see the organization and its needs with more clarity and insight because your interactions are focused, and the primary purpose is to seek out stories and listen."

I was like a schoolboy captivated by the subject my teacher was teaching. Vivian confided in me the secrets to implementing leaning in and removing barriers. She practically whispered forcing me to lean in and focus on her every word.

"We are inundated with noise and distractions. I'm sure you've experienced this as a leader. Sometimes it seems nearly impossible to free ourselves from the things demanding our attention. People are the least of our distractions, truth be told. We need to discipline ourselves to give our team members our undivided attention. Look people in the eye. We listen best with our eyes wide-open. Our eyes are emblematic of what's going on inside our hearts. Focusing in with our eyes and hearts is a powerful magnet for connecting with people.

"Put down your phone. Turn off or put your computer on sleep. Slow the pace of the conversation. Engage people one-on-one. In meetings, look at the person who is speaking and set the expectations at the beginning. Let team members know that interruptions are not acceptable. Ask that everyone respects the speaker and allows them to finish.

"One way to help those who can't help themselves and must interrupt is to ask everyone to write down their thoughts so they can be addressed later in the meeting. Also, make sure everyone's phone is on silent, not vibrate, or off. Disconnect Bluetooth settings so watches aren't buzzing. Another option is, no phones during meetings."

I checked my phone at that moment. It was on silent, but my watch buzzed with a notification. I looked away sheepishly to turn Bluetooth off on my phone.

"There's a manager we worked with who would rarely close her laptop during most of her one-on-one meetings. She'd nod her head and smile as updates were shared. But it was obvious she was practicing what we call distracted listening. It was affecting her relationships with the people she led and the projects she managed. She came to talk with us about the disconnect.

"With our encouragement she implemented the principle to lean in and remove barriers. After she began closing her laptop, stopped checking her phone during meetings, and started looking right at people when they were talking, her team members began getting something out of the meetings and productivity and creativity blossomed. They began to connect with her. She heard from the team that many felt as if they were accomplishing much more because of their conversations with her."

Vivian stopped to reach for her tea then turned toward the counter and asked Luca for a refill. The lesson continued while Cecile sat quietly and observed.

"The culture of her organization shifted, and the disconnection dissipated. This simple adjustment in communication made a difference. Someone else was responsible for taking accurate notes in every meeting and distributing them to all who attended. She could now give her undivided attention. Does any of this sound familiar?"

"Sounds like me with my assistant, Melody. She's always in our meetings taking notes, but I take my own notes. Duplicating efforts, right? She probably feels like I don't trust her."

Vivian and Cecile nodded affirming my observation. I started to think about my inefficiency and asked myself why my daily routine felt so full.

This time Cecile leaned in; her clear blue eyes capturing my attention. "Here's another way to lean in and remove barriers. Include people who don't instinctively speak up in meetings. Directly, by name, ask for their opinions. Over time, they will feel comfortable sharing. You will have established the expectation that all who are in a meeting will contribute. You will reinforce that their thoughts and ideas are valuable. All people need encouragement.

"We can't ignore the introverts. They are often deeper wells of insight than we realize. In a society where 75% of us are extroverted, introverts tend to be overlooked. Trust me, I have been overlooked often in meetings. To this day, I try my best to pay attention to our quiet colleagues to help them feel safe and valued."

I was thinking about Cesar, the comptroller, who was one of the most reliable employees we have. But he never spoke up. He managed our finances and must have insight for how to be more efficient and save money.

"Early on in my career I learned from a wonderful mentor about removing barriers between the people I would meet and me," the light musical lilt of Cecile's voice broke into my thoughts. "He would never sit behind his desk. He always pulled up a chair in front of me so that we were sitting with nothing between us."

I recalled my intention to do this with Jaime and the disaster that ensued.

"It was a powerful symbol. When someone with whom you are speaking sits behind a big desk, it can feel imposing. Consider it a powerplay. Sitting behind the desk symbolizes dominance and creates an imbalance in the conversation. Always meet with people from a position of equality and respect. Create an atmosphere for a more relational dialogue.

"I stopped sitting behind a desk in meetings. I also stopped sitting at the head of the conference table. Instead, I sit in the middle of one side or the other or I go to whatever seat is open when I arrive. If our meeting space were big enough, we would install a round table to remove the concept familiar in hierarchical organizations of the leader sitting in a place of distinction.

"My desk now faces the wall. Yes, my back is to the door, but I have created more space in the room and removed the barrier," Cecile leaned back, and I followed suit. "I realize we have been doing most of the talking today. As we continue, we will talk less and model the LISTEN acronym more. For now, this is more than a listening session. We are here to offer insight and training.

"Leaders sometimes need to be reminded of who they know they can be or taught a new approach to leadership. We think you sit in the former group. But just in case, we want to be sure we address the latter as well. This is not about us," Cecile waved her hand from Vivian to herself then, palm up, she gestured toward me. "It is about you."

"I really appreciate this," I told them and expressed my gratitude for those simple and effective tips. "You're not talking too much. I know I will have a lot more to say next week."

I continued, "I'm beginning to understand ***L*** *– lean in and remove barriers.* I've done some of your tips at work and at home without realizing it. I recognized from our first meeting how you leaned in and removed barriers from our conversation. When you were directly in front of me, so close I thought our noses would touch, I didn't understand. That simple uncomfortable act had great impact." Vivian and Cecile gave each other a knowing look and smiled.

"I feel much more comfortable coming to you to ask questions, confess mistakes, and admit how often I don't know what to do. I feel respected by you which helps me feel safe in our conversations. The fact that you do what you say is important. I'm experiencing the principles first-hand and it's encouraging. What you're saying is making sense. I'm excited to learn more!"

"So, we're on for next week?," Vivian asked as she started to put on her hot pink rain boots.

"You bet we are. You've given me so much to think about. I can't wait to hear what's next!"

"Same here. Homework time. Practice ***L*** *– lean in and remove barriers.* Get comfortable with being uncomfortable. Look people in the eye and set the expectation at meetings that interruptions won't be accepted. Okay?," I didn't get the chance to answer. It was obvious the only acceptable response would be *Yes.*

"Time for us to go see our families." Cecile gave me a quick hug and was on her way. Following close behind were the hot pink rubber boots squeaking with each step.

Before I left, I went to find Luca to ask about the test. She was able to take a break and we spoke for about fifteen minutes. I practiced leaning in and removing barriers. I listened with intention. It was an exhilarating exercise and I left feeling like I had made a difference in one person's life – by listening.

Later that day, sitting in my office, I kept shaking my head. I guess I had too much time to think about my meeting with Cecile and Vivian. I began to rationalize all of it. *It couldn't be that easy, could it? Simply listening to Jaime and other employees, family and friends, neighbors, and strangers? Had I been absent by not applying such a simple principle all along?* I realized I wasn't alone in my feelings. I knew of many other leaders who had things backwards, speaking twice as much as they listen. After all, that was conventional wisdom in the world of management.

And then there was the 2by2 concept and being a story seeker. Who would I partner with? Could we afford to implement such a practice? Would Jaime be the right person to discuss this with? Would I find the stories I listened to interesting?

"But I don't have time to listen," I rationalized out loud. "I need to keep running the company. After all, the proverbial buck ultimately stops with me."

The reality of hearing an enticing theory and putting it into practice was hitting me hard. "What about my authority? Won't *my* authority be threatened if people perceive listening is all I do or that I'm looking for others' ideas and suggestions too often? Won't *I* be considered weak and not a good manager or leader? Also, I don't like the thought of having to change my management style. After all, it's taken the company this far! Why do I need to know more about my employees? I pay them well."

My mind would not slow down as I sat in my office. I forgot to set up my meeting with Melody to refine my calendar. Then I remembered she has a business degree. Marathon and business degree. I have to ask her about both.

I had never made the connection before, but it seemed obvious, in my weakest moment, the way I was being at work is the same way I was being at home. For years my wife had stated that I hadn't been present, truly present, with her, our girls, and many others. That everything revolved around work. That I wasn't listening and didn't seem to care about those I loved and appreciated the most. That they were last on my priority list.

I began to sense my pattern at work was also my pattern at home. And things weren't going so well at either place. It was becoming clearer how something needed to change.

I packed up my backpack and left. I told Melody I would be gone for the day and asked her to reschedule my appointments. She tried to protest, but I kept walking. And, no, I never asked her about the marathon training.

LEAN IN AND REMOVE BARRIERS

Eliminate distractions

Look people in the eye

Put technology away

Encourage the introverts

Remove barriers

“I”
INTERESTED AND CURIOUS

We live in a world that is hyper-connected technologically,

yet extremely disconnected relationally.

We met again the following week at the same coffee shop. I was dragging my body through the door. My mind still at home. Cecile sat alone this time at the table in the far corner still arriving before me even though I was 10 minutes early. As soon as she saw me enter, she closed her lap-top and put away her phone. It was obvious that she made our time together a priority.

As I approached the table, she stood and pulled me in offering a European greeting by kissing me on both cheeks. I was getting used to the hugs, this was a change. After we caught up on the past week for a few minutes, I asked about Vivian.

"She is going to be tardy today. About thirty minutes," her blues eyes twinkled, and the pink lipstick enhanced her smile. "So, are you ready for round two? Or is it three? You look a bit groggy, how are you today?" She leaned in, eyes wide open, genuinely interested.

"To be honest, I'm a bit overwhelmed. We had a rough strategy meeting yesterday afternoon. We are, again, a bit behind in the first quarter of the year. And on top of that, one of my daughters is sick. She was up most of the night. I tried to give Amanda a much-needed night off, so I was up several times throughout the night.

"And then there is this pandemic. We are trying to wrap our heads around that whole debacle and understand how it will affect our day-to-day operations."

"Ah, yes. That is a dilemma. We are experiencing the same. But I suspect our company may have an easier adjustment with our employees since most work remotely already. What we are thinking about is how we will communicate with clients. So, I empathize with what you are dealing with. And thank you for your honesty. I must admit, it was a thoughtful thing you did for your wife and I'm sure she appreciated it very much. I hope your daughter is doing better today."

"She is. Thanks. If you don't mind, I'd like to get started before Vivian arrives. I'm tired and feeling off-balance. But this is important. We've only discussed the first letter of the acronym and I am fighting the change."

"Okay. Tell me what's going on and then we'll talk about ***I*** *– Interested and Curious*."

I explained to her how I started to rationalize my role once I returned to the office. I had already been implementing ***L*** *– lean in and remove barriers*, by being intentional, leaning in physically, making eye contact, and removing barriers. I even moved my desk which was the most difficult act. I didn't realize how safe I felt sitting behind it. There was no symbol of authority left between me and the other person. Then my fear of becoming irrelevant started to take over.

"Why does it seem like being a good listener is a weakness?"

"That is a misperception informed by your history as a manager and reinforced in formal business education and within the business world – especially in the West. You have managed systems, processes, projects, and even people. But have you been a leader? Leaders understand that listening is a strength."

"Managing and leading. Aren't they the same thing?"

Before she could answer, Vivian joined us apologizing profusely for being late. She didn't appear to be her normal upbeat, put-together self. I suspected there was something wrong. Probably issues with the pandemic – just like what we were all facing. She sat down and listened while Cecile answered my question.

"They overlap, yes. But not everyone who manages is a leader. And not every leader is a manager. Being a leader is about people. Leaders exist within and outside of business and organizations. Management skills are developed and possessed by many but being able to manage does not necessarily have to include interacting with people."

"Hmm, you mean the lady at my church who keeps trying to ask me how I'm doing may be an example of a leader?"

"Sure. She may be an example of someone who is known as a servant leader. They don't have to be in the foreground of situations. They don't have to manage or lead an organization. They have a way about them that allows for the development and support of other people. They don't need to be recognized. Servant leaders also exist within those who are CEOs, pastors, team leaders, on sports teams, and other vocations in which the person accepts the responsibility of an organization and its people. The difference is those leaders understand the importance of lifting up others, so each becomes the best version of themselves."

I sat listening, simply listening.

"Is this making sense?"

I nodded.

"Not everyone is a servant leader. There are other leadership styles out there. Some may be perceived as better than others. In some organizations, the person at the helm may need develop and incorporate a style of leadership other than a servant leader. Perhaps more directive. What you will need to determine within the organization for which you are responsible, is whether it is ready for a servant leader. Does the purpose and structure of the organization support and have room for this leadership style?" They paused to let that question sink in. Complete silence.

"The one thing leadership has at its core is people. Leaning in and removing barriers invites people to participate. And ***I*** – *interested and curious*, which we are going to discuss, helps you to become informed and observant. As the CEO, while you are transforming who you are as a leader and the culture of your company, the old way of perceiving what a manager is and does will creep in. What you must consciously do is acknowledge it and then move on. Don't allow the old way of being stop you from opening lines of communication with your employees. Growth, adapting, and transformation has a place in organizations as well as families.

"Implementing LISTEN into your leadership style improves your disposition and your influence. By extension, you help to make your business better and stronger. And, today, you help to create one that can withstand a pandemic."

"I'm beginning to understand. But based on some of the conversations we've had, you can imagine my insecurities will cause me to be a bit wary of change. Modeling and expressing my ideas and new way of being to our team leaders based on the principles of LISTEN is discomforting."

"That is also understandable. Remember what we said, get comfortable with being uncomfortable. There is a reason you are the leader. We just want to work together on growing your leadership capacity by improving your listening abilities. Understand, it is just as important for you to be able to express your creative ideas as it is for anyone else to express theirs."

Nearly 30 minutes had passed, and we hadn't even begun to move the discussion to ***I*** *– interested and curious*. After what felt like a long awkward silence, Vivian suggested we move on to ***I*** to see if that will help me continue my forward momentum toward my transformation as a leader.

"Let's come back to your concern about presenting your creative ideas," she said. "It shows solid self-awareness on your part, knowing when to speak and when to listen. When you have a good idea, a creative one, and you share it with others, what makes you feel appreciated?"

"Hmm. I guess it's when others communicate that they have not only listened to the idea, but are genuinely interested," I answered. "And on top of that, once the idea has been implemented and it makes a significant difference, an improvement, I hope my contribution is recognized."

"Exactly!"

"I know I surprised some people, but everyone who came in and sat down to talk commented how much they liked the new layout of my office and especially the new feel of it. They seemed more relaxed. I started to feel more relaxed too. I liked it. I'd never thought about that kind of arrangement before. I had conversations and didn't give lectures. I prepared for the meetings by having questions. When the meetings were spontaneous, I started by listening, being a story seeker – even if it was a micro story. Questions to dig deeper into the topic seemed to come easier, not perfect, but easier than before. Last week validated my plan to try out other tools to develop as a listener and story seeker. It's kind of energizing to try them and see what positive things might begin to take place.

"Conversations were more open and free-flowing. I leaned in and intentionally listened. I was interested in what everyone who came in had to say."

"That's it. Without realizing it, you were applying ***I*** *– interested and curious*. I noticed as I was leaving the shop last week that you took the time to talk with Luca. Again, you were interested and curious. Curiosity almost demands an inquisitive mind. You told us you asked more questions, even during spontaneous meetings. Did they require yes/no responses, or did you ask open-ended questions? As you listened, did you recognize the strengths of those you spoke with? Remember the story about the Alaskan huskies?"

"As I think about it, I did ask more questions but probably got more yes/no responses. I admit, I'm still a little overwhelmed. As the CEO, I should know how to do this stuff, right? I feel like I'm supposed to know so I can provide guidance, not ask questions.

"Jaime is probably my best role model and my nemesis wrapped up in one person. Even though I know she is an excellent manager – I mean, leader and manager – I also know she could easily do my job. Maybe that's why I feel threatened and have been dismissive when she speaks."

"Great personal observation," Vivian said. "This is normal. Many people continue to work in the old paradigm of top-down management. *Be seen and not heard* – the same adage used on children. When this dismissive reaction has happened to you, how have you felt and reacted?"

"Worthless, unappreciated, like I would never improve or be promoted. At home, I see it with my kids when I tell them I'll get to them as soon as I finish an email or make a phone call. Their shoulders slump and they hang their heads as they turn to walk away. There must be a different way employees shoulder slump and hang their heads."

"Tell me what you think that is."

"Well, if I think about Jaime, she gave me an ultimatum. What she did up to that point, I don't know because I wasn't interested. I just wanted her to do her job. I think the first time I saw Melody smile was the day she told me about her marathon training. Now that I think about it, she would normally duck in and out of my office as quickly as possible. I didn't know she was a marathon runner."

I stared at my full teacup, now cold.

Vivian and Cecile sat in silence waiting for me to continue.

Time ticked by before Cecile broke the silence. "A leader expresses genuine interest in and is curious about others' hopes, dreams, and visions for the organization and for the personal lives of those they lead," she began. "Acknowledge what they say. Respond positively to their needs and desires, to their ideas. They will trust you, begin to express their thoughts, and respect you more and more.

"Let me give an example. Let's say you went to the meeting yesterday afternoon, knowing the company is behind in the first quarter, and you presented your ideas of how the company might get out of the hole. How do you think the others in the team would have reacted?"

I sat in silence pondering the question. "Honestly, there may have been two reactions. They could have been surprised that I had ideas or there could have been a feeling that my directive nature was overbearing, and no other ideas would be considered."

"Okay. Now consider another approach. What if you started the meeting asking for the ideas from those who were there with you, your teammates? What if you served as the scribe at the white board and listened to each one of them express their ideas? How much would that change things?"

Silence again on my part. "Well," I began, "I suppose the reaction would have been similar. Surprise and… silence. I say silence because that is not how our meetings work. I do most of the talking."

"Okay. Now think about one more approach. What if you encouraged the group to take a time-out, grab a whiteboard, quiet their minds, and record their thoughts. Here is what this interchange might look like when it is working well.

"You start by saying, *I know we are in a bit of a financial crunch right now. I'd like to give all of you the floor here. This is a team effort, and the company needs your input and ideas. Using the white boards on the walls, on your own or in teams, brainstorm how we can improve our performance in the second quarter. Talk about how we will address the pandemic if we must close our doors. Be prepared to discuss this. Let's take about 15 minutes to brainstorm then genuinely listen to each other's ideas. Let's find the solution together.*

"After all participants have shared their ideas, and this includes you, Jeffrey, it's time to eliminate what truly won't work to get to the heart of the conversation and come up with real solutions."

"Don't be offended if your ideas aren't selected. This is part of the growth and transformation for you, those on your team, and the organization," Vivian emphasized. "You're building trust and respect. This is where you have a focused opportunity to practice ***I*** *– interested and curious*."

"I didn't do that last week. Remember I mentioned Cesar, the comptroller. Well, he's also an introvert. When he tried to bring up some ideas for change while we were meeting one-on-one, I completely dismissed him."

"Let me throw this out for you to consider," said Vivian. "You were in that meeting alone with Cesar. If you had had someone else there with you, a counterbalance, do you think he would have been able to express his ideas fully?"

"Well, maybe. I don't know. Frankly, there is no one I trusted or knew who could partner with me for these types of conversations."

"What about Jaime?"

I glanced at Vivian. I know my expression was one of disbelief. "Why would I consider Jaime? She is threatening to leave the company."

"Part of our responsibility as listeners," Vivian explained, "is to help you hear what you have said out loud, what is left unsaid, and what you have expressed through your body language. This is why we encourage Listening 2by2 as a leadership tool.

"When it comes to Jaime, you have not expressed anything negative about her performance. You have told us you admire her for how she leads. Apart from feeling perhaps jealous and even a little threatened by her, you have acknowledged that she has put her work, direct-reports, team, and the company first. You have acknowledged an appreciation for how she communicates with others in the company and seems to know something personal about each person she meets. Would you agree?"

I nodded while I stared at my teacup.

"There comes a time when you have to let your guard down, be vulnerable. Put your pride and ego aside and ask for help. Trust me, I know all about pride and having a big ego," Vivian declared, and Cecile nodded enthusiastically in agreement.

"I used to run around telling everyone what to do. Explaining how they were wrong and then fixing everything myself. Cecile was, and is, a lot like Jaime. Caring, a natural teacher, hard-worker, and a calming presence. I admired her style from afar, but it took me at least a year to finally ask her for help. It was at that point when we started to develop the Listening 2by2 leadership concept.

"When an employee would come in for a performance review, for example, we always explained why there were two of us present. It wasn't to intimidate the employee. It was to be sure we were listening. Where one may have been actively listening or observing body language, the other would enter the conversation by asking probing questions or acknowledging our employee's concerns by answering questions."

I sat still reflecting on my leadership style and considering how to approach Jaime – if I were to approach her.

My listeners glanced at each other, and Cecile picked up where Vivian left off.

"Consider what Vivian just shared. It is not a leadership and management approach that is widespread. As a matter of fact, we know of no other organization outside of ours that does this. They may exist, we simply are not aware of them. Think about this as a way to have a partner who will carry some of the load. Jaime may not be the CEO, and that's okay. She is a significant member of the leadership team. This concept is easily adapted in all forms of organizational structures and sizes. Just consider working with Jaime, for now. Let's go back to discussing ***I*** *– interested and curious.*

"This is hypothetical. Let's say your idea is to hire another sales rep and you present it to the HR team. Team members respond by saying *We heard you and think your idea is important. You are correct that, on paper, it doesn't make sense to grow the team. However, let's see how and if we can make it work.* Then Cesar speaks up and raises a concern. What do you do?"

I didn't want to respond with the obvious *let him speak*, so I sat in silence. In truth, I probably would have dismissed him again.

"Does that exchange make sense?," Vivian asked.

"It does," I responded. "But it sounds too perfect. Especially if I'm trying to get their input. And, as for Cesar, I would probably dismiss him again. I feel terrible admitting that."

Smiling, Vivian said, "Listeners don't discourage ideas. Listeners ask good, probing questions to discover more good ideas. Practice being interested and curious. Not every idea is valid and doable, but every idea is worth hearing. We'll come back to your response about Cesar."

"Let me ask you another question," Cecile interjected. "How much would that conversation change your leadership style? What would getting their input do for the culture of your company? As for Cesar, how much effort would it take for you to stop, listen, engage, and consider his contribution? When you practice participatory leadership, the self-worth of each employee is reinforced. It is important for each member of a team to understand that they are as important as the person, or persons, in the C-Suite. If you want to be an effective leader, you have to listen."

"My head is about to explode… in a good way. You've given me so much to reflect upon and to put into action. I'm already looking forward to the next letter in the acronym, ***S*** *– Simplify and Self-Care*," I said.

"My friend, you're proving that you are a great listener. Great listeners are great learners," Vivian tapped my knee with her spoon and made sure I looked directly at her.

She continued, "There is always more to learn, so let's keep listening and learning together. Time to go be with our family," she abruptly exclaimed. "We'll see you next week as long as the pandemic doesn't cause business to shut down. If it does, we'll call you to set up a meeting to discuss how and when we'll meet. Together, just like we have been discussing today, we'll come up with a solution. We are committed to work with you. Same time? Same place?"

Like the wind, they were off to be with family. We finished right on time. It was 9 a.m. and I couldn't help but wonder how they were able to be with family at that time of the day and not at work. Well, I had to be at my office, so I gathered my things, said good-bye to the people who worked in the coffee shop (also something new for me), and walked to work.

INTERESTED AND CURIOUS

Be open to learning from everyone

Invite others' ideas, visions, and dreams

Acknowledge others' perspectives

Ask probing questions

Respond positively to others' input

"S"

SIMPLIFY AND SELF-CARE

Effective leaders are the best listeners. They don't discourage creativity, in fact, just the opposite, they encourage it.

I plopped into the seat at our regular table. I was feeling horrible but didn't want to miss our meeting. I didn't have to go to the counter anymore, which felt awesome! Today, Luca stopped by our table and asked if I wanted to try some ginger tea. "It will help with whatever you have."

I didn't have the strength to argue and agreed with a nod. Vivian and Cecile looked a little uncomfortable. I just brushed it off and smiled.

"How's your daughter doing?," Vivian asked.

"Much, much better. Thanks for asking. It's me, now. I don't think it's contagious."

Cecile gave Vivian a concerned glance. "You have been reading about the pandemic, right?"

"Absolutely. It's confusing information we are receiving."

"Yes it is. I'm sure you won't mind; we are keeping our masks on. Even though we aren't six feet apart, Vivian and I make sure we have the filter inserts. If you would please keep yours on except when you take a sip of tea, we would appreciate it. Let's continue for this week," Cecile encouraged. "We'll see what we have to do about next week when the time comes. This fits in well with our talk today about ***S*** - *simplify and self-care*. You know there is technology out there so we can meet using the computers," her mask concealed her smile.

"I didn't think about it with us, but we have been discussing it at work. I thought we had to meet in person. I'll keep that in mind if I'm still under the weather next week." I pulled out my handkerchief and coughed into it even through my mask.

"Sounds like a bad chest cold. Do you feel up to this?"

"Yes, please. I really need to talk."

"Hmm, okay. But we will cut this short if you think you need to leave." I nodded that I would let them know.

"How are the company's financial statements for the second quarter beginning to look?," Vivian asked.

Listening never seemed to end for her. She wanted to know more and more about me and my situation. Story seeker in the flesh.

"It's still slow. The pandemic has not helped. I know it's going to take some time. The good news is we've begun listening more to one another and are deciding on the best plan of action - together!," Jeffrey attempted a smile.

Cecile clapped her hands and smiled. "You are correct. Creating a culture you're looking for is going to take time. So, before we continue discussing ***S***, what reflections did you have after last week?"

"Cesar has been a godsend. I admit I haven't always taken the time to show much interest in others' ideas over the years. But I was thrilled to listen last week. You're helping me to think more about how taking the time to be genuinely interested in hearing others' stories, vision, and thoughts is vital."

I had to blow my nose. Luca arrived with my tea and some honey, and I thanked her profusely and complimented her *dia de los muertos*-themed mask. It was colorful and quite beautiful. She smiled and told me she would tell her mother how much I liked it.

Vivian and Cecile sat patiently completely unaffected by the honking noise from across the table. Taking my first sip of tea I realized how much I cut back on coffee. I smiled inside because my face wouldn't cooperate.

"I think when I've felt especially insecure about my position as a leader, I've had a tendency to believe that soliciting others' opinions would show me as being indecisive or weak, that I couldn't figure everything out for myself. To be honest, so much of the modeling I've observed over the years taught me that - don't share doubts, don't appear as if you don't have ready answers for problems, don't admit to not knowing something or to making a mistake."

The tea warmed my chest, and the honey was the perfect amount of sweet.

"That was an old-school model," I continued. "But I'm hearing and learning at work, and by coincidence from others outside of work, that we need to be more open today. It's healthier and it can ultimately make the organization stronger. This pandemic and the looming shut down is bringing communication – listening – to the top of everyone's list of priorities and skills to develop. As I've said, I've never been good at asking questions, showing interest in what others might be thinking, expressing vulnerability. I thought it showed weakness as a leader. It really is a strength. After all, I'm listening to the two of you," I smiled, unhooked my mask and took a sip of tea.

"Listening and story seeking can help to make the company stronger. It also might lift the burden from me to have every answer and every idea. I've recognized the strong executive team of gifted individuals I am surrounded by. We share a common goal. This isn't a solo act, and I'm working hard to remember that. I'm grateful that my eyes and mind are being opened to this. It's healthier and I'm starting to see it. And you know, I realize I'm being more intentional about listening at home, too."

"Our health, physical and mental, is vital for us to be our best selves," Vivian added.

"When you talk about simplifying your schedule for better listening and reflection, I struggle. I just feel as if I don't have time for that. The demands are relentless and I'm always feeling pressure to perform," I bemoaned. "Help me here. And self-care. Seriously. What does that look like for a person in my shoes?"

"Did you ever have that sit down with Melody to go over your calendar?"

"No. I still haven't done that."

"Jeffrey," Vivian's tone was kind but firm. She moved to the edge of her seat, and I was positive she could see the snot coursing through my nostrils.

"Before you do, determine your priorities and set boundaries. When you do, you'll find that you have more time in the day than you think. Melody will be your protector, your gatekeeper. You're describing a very common frustration. The most successful leaders have the same demands. But they understand that listening to their team members must be scheduled too. This is part of leading people and managing assets. In this case the asset is time. Listening is just as essential and valuable as anything else."

"In fact," Cecile was speaking now, "you will come to realize that when you listen to understand what others need to do their jobs effectively, your schedule begins to open up. You become more confident in others and trust their capabilities so delegating responsibilities is easier. Conflicts are lessened. More problems are resolved. Productivity and results increase. Satisfaction and pride in accomplishments is heightened."

"Top performing and effective leaders don't book the entire day," Vivian now. "They *delegate* what they don't need to do. They realize they can't do it all and shouldn't. They trust others to get the job done instilling confidence and commitment. They work smarter, not harder. They concentrate on what *they* need to do and allow others to do the balance."

Before me was a lesson in how to be part of a tag team.

Cecile, "The space leaders gain by simplifying enables them to give others their full attention. It gives them time to reflect more fully as well as think through and respond to challenges and ideas. I have found that I listen more and listen better when I create space in my day. When I have back-to-back meetings, my goal is mainly to get through them with just enough time to run to my next meeting.

"When I strategically simplify, I create time in between meetings to be able to reflect on a conversation and prepare for the next one so I am always present. This is where Melody will become your biggest advocate and your conscience.

"Sometimes, as you rightly noted, it's less that we don't want to listen, it's more the case that we don't have the space to intentionally listen. I made it a practice at home years ago to communicate to my family when I am not available, except for emergencies. I intentionally set aside time and space so I can listen better to my family. They get my undivided attention. Tell me, Jeffrey, what can you do?"

I needed a few minutes to think. My head was pounding, my nose was runny, and my body ached but I didn't want to walk away just yet.

"First, I can employ, no pun intended, Melody. She can keep track of my time at work and remind me of my priorities, especially with my family. For example, I can explain to anyone who stops by for a chat, or what they consider to be urgent, that I really want to hear from them, but at that moment, I can't.

"I can let them know they can check with Melody to see when I have time. I want to be able to clear my head before I go home so I am present for my family. So, using drive time to meet with someone spur-of-the-moment by phone is off-limits. Like you said, emergencies are the exception. Just going through that scenario, I am realizing how valuable Melody is to my simplifying my schedule."

"Beautifully expressed, Jeffrey. Now what about self-care?"

"What about it?"

"That's the other half of ***S*** *– simplify and self-care*. What are you doing to take care of yourself?," Vivian asked. "How long has it been since you have had a physical?"

"I don't know." I was a little soft around the middle, but not unhealthy.

"Well, that begs the question, Jeffrey. Where should you start?," Cecile inquired.

Silence. Silence so thick you could cut it with a knife. My mind was searching for a response. I haven't thought about my health in a long time. I subconsciously touched my side, my chest, and my head. Where has the time gone?

Vivian and Cecile sat quietly waiting for me to process the concept of self-care. I would find out later that this was a part of the listening process. Silence can be revealing, revolutionary, and – at least right now – annoying. I kept searching for my answer and it finally came to me.

Stuttering, hoping this was what they wanted to hear, I finally spoke, "I suppose I could make an appointment with my doctor for a physical." I ended the statement on a high note as though I were asking a question.

"If that's what you think you need to do, then that's where you need to start," Vivian was encouraging and gave me no indication that I had hit upon the "right" answer. "You need to have a starting point to determine how to take care of your body. Promise us you will arrive next week – pandemic shutdown pending – or send us an email to let us know you have an appointment on the calendar."

"I will," my inner child responded.

"I think we have been here long enough. You've toughed it out and need to go home, or to the doctor."

As soon as Cecile said that I felt the weight of my symptoms and my body slumped. "You're right. Thank you for today. This is helping me so much. But right now, I do need to go."

"Okay. Don't worry about this, we'll take care of everything."

I smiled weakly and dragged my body toward the door. I couldn't even look back to wave goodbye. I just wanted to go to bed.

The following week I received an email from Vivian and Cecile:

We hope you are feeling better. Did you go to the doctor? What did you have? We hope it wasn't the virus. Please let us know how you are. We'd like to know when we can meet again. We know this shutdown is affecting everyone, but we don't want to stop our meetings. Maybe postpone them for a few weeks? Obviously, we can't meet in person. What do you propose? Here, we are already using Zoom to do our meetings. Is your company on Zoom? How are your employees? This is crazy... We hope you are well.

Vivian and Cecile

I sat back in my seat, this time at my desk in my makeshift home office, preparing to reply. This lockdown has opened my eyes to what I have been taking for granted and we are only at the beginning of it. What will happen next?

I explained to them that I was doing well. Just a regular 24-hour flu. I reassured them that I had made my appointment with my doctor for a physical but since we can no longer meet in person for routine appointments, I wasn't sure it would happen. I made a plan, I told them. Starting at home, I would do daily sit ups and pushups.

My kids and wife pointed out that there were plenty of YouTube videos of workouts I could follow. "Going to get up an hour early and do at least thirty minutes every day," I declared.

They wrote back that they understood and included, *Jeffrey, can we negotiate when to meet again? We think it's important to have this on your calendar and ours. Also, can we make it a two-hour meeting?"*

Let's do it! I replied. *I'll make sure Melody blocks off the time. We'll explore **T** – Talk Less and Embrace Silence and **E** – Explain and Ask Questions, right? Expect an email from Melody with dates/times when I am available. She may send an appointment link, so you have more options.*

They responded:

*Yes, **T** and **E**. We hope you recognize this time at home as an opportunity to truly listen to your family and the ones closest to you. The best listening begins at home, doesn't it? Enjoy the time and space away from the building you called 'work' and your 'office'. Remember to listen to yourself too. All the best until next time!*

Vivian and Cecile

Our next meeting was on the calendar. In the meantime, I worked on ***L*** through ***S***.

SIMPLIFY AND SELF-CARE

Care for yourself

Prioritize listening

Delegate what others can do better than you

Create intentional space to be fully engaged

"T"
TALK LESS AND EMBRACE SILENCE

Go heavy on silence, light on advice. You don't need to fix everyone's problems. Most of us don't enjoy being told what to do; we prefer being shown what to do and coming to our own conclusions.

It took us two months before we were able to coordinate our next meeting. I was so happy to have the conversation and see their faces – even over Zoom. We still had tea, too. Vivian said she wasn't feeling 100% and asked if we could keep this to an hour instead of two. We all agreed. I was a little concerned since the virus was affecting people about her age. She reassured me that it was nothing serious.

"I'm sorry you aren't feeling well. It means a lot to me that you'd continue to give your time on a day like today," I shared.

For the next five minutes I listened to Vivian describe how sick she was and how distressing it was to not have her family over and be able to truly enjoy the time together. I listened and only spoke to express empathy at moments when she took a break. She needed to be heard just as I need to be heard, just as everyone needs to be heard.

"Thanks, Jeffrey. You are evolving as a listener! Are you ready to discuss ***T*** – *Talk Less and Embrace Silence*? First thing though, let's talk about your reflections from the past two months. We've received a few emails from you but nothing consistent. You've been proactive about considering all that we've talked about, right? Let's hear what you've been thinking and doing."

Cecile never spoke a word throughout the meeting. It was obvious she was concerned for her best friend. Perhaps she felt it would serve her well to let her take the lead for today. It was as if the exercise of having to listen and respond helped Vivian get through the hour. I was in awe of how the two were in tune with each other. I hoped I would find a similar friendship. And develop this awareness with my wife and children.

"Oh, sure! I'm ready to learn about both the letters ***T*** and ***E***! Well, only ***T*** today since it's obvious you need to leave early. But first, I do want to tell you what I'm excited about from our last meeting.

"Here's the background. One of the reasons I'm filled with such angst about Jaime leaving, besides the fact that she's our best leader, is that last year we also lost a top manager to another organization. He left on fairly good terms to accept a position where the pay was better, and he could work the majority of time from home. Well, because we had been in a financial crunch and needed to save money, I decided not to fill the position. I thought we might be able to absorb it and divide the responsibilities. It was also a job I held several years ago. I knew what needed to be done and began absorbing it into my schedule and portfolio."

I could see the question they both had.

"No, I didn't divide the responsibilities. I did pretty well with it at first and used the money the company saved to justify my decision. The fact that I could do it more easily than just about anyone else in the organization seemed to also reinforce the choice I made. The problem was, or still is, that in doing someone else's job, I wasn't doing justice to mine. It's a huge reason why I'm so overwhelmed and stressed. I'm not taking the time to listen to others because I'm trying to cross off the tasks on my "to do" list.

"The challenge to *simplify* and remember *self-care* really hit home with me the last couple of weeks. I realized I needed to stop doing that other job so I could get back to doing mine. I had to force myself to practice intentionally listening to our team members and worked hard to build trust."

They both nodded and encouraged me to continue.

"Last week, I called a meeting with all the managers, including Jaime. I told them I could no longer do both jobs. I apologized for taking on more than I should have and confessed that I needed their help. I asked for their ideas about how we could address the issue and the vacant position. I posed questions like

Do we simply need to hire someone, bite the bullet and take a risk to spend the money? Can we break up the position into different departments and share the responsibilities? Is there someone in the company who we can promote who has the gift and skills to handle all aspects of the job? I asked them to dream and to consider the risks.

"Then Jaime spoke up, *What about Melody?* I stopped in my tracks. *What about her?* Jaime laid out all her credentials. How she knew, I don't know. Well, I should know by now. Jaime knows everyone. I asked everyone to consider promoting Melody and the other ideas we discussed. Truthfully, I needed to think it through too. Melody and I have been working well together since I finally asked her to help me with my schedule.

"We made no decisions that day, except that I needed to simplify my schedule by letting go of that position. I listened to them. I want to continue listening to them and am prioritizing the time to do it. We meet again next week and we're going to continue meeting until we have a plan and can implement it.

"I went home that night and discussed the dilemma with Amanda. She was thrilled that I asked for her perspective and input. She thought promoting Melody was a great idea and suggested I discuss it with her. The only requirement before she left the position would be that she had to train her replacement. I had not discussed it with Melody yet because I didn't want to give her a false sense of possibility. I decided to discuss it with the team first and hear their feedback.

"Unfortunately, Jaime spoke with her about the prospect of a promotion. I found out the Monday after our meeting when Melody let me know she was interested. Here was an opportunity to have another listening session with Jaime. I asked her why she discussed it with Melody. Her explanation was adequate. I talked less and let her explain. Then it was my turn, and I was able to explain why what she did was not appropriate or her responsibility. She had set expectations that may not be the solution."

"Wow!" exclaimed Vivian. "I'm incredibly proud of you for this. "Simplify", to begin to listen with intention. You're really starting to do it."

"As a manager and leader, as I told you earlier, I've always felt as if I am supposed to have a lot to say when others come to me," I continued. "That I'm supposed to have all the answers. Or that I need to critique what they are telling me. I now realize there's another way to think about that."

"You're learning quickly," Vivian chuckled. "I also want to point out that you used principles ***T** – Talk Less and Embrace Silence* and ***E** – Explain and Ask Questions*. Did you realize that?"

"No! But I'm glad something's sinking in," I laughed. "Maybe I *am* able to change, to go through a transformation."

We were halfway through the LISTEN acronym. Finally, I was beginning to feel as if I were catching on. Committing to the practice of listening was step number one. It helped to have the principles to follow and apply.

"Most of us jump in too quickly," she began. "We only hear a few thoughts and then we hijack the conversation. What I've found to help the most is to listen without jumping in so fast and without jumping to conclusions and interpreting what you hear right away. Doing so short-circuits the dialogue. We don't have to be so quick to pronounce a solution.

"Often, others aren't looking for us to provide an answer. They simply want to be heard and to have their experience acknowledged. Sometimes there is no answer or solution. Many times, the person knows what to do, even if they resist having to do it. Most times they're merely seeking to vent. Other times they're asking for advice and want to hear your thoughts. But it's best to ask them directly if they want your input if you're not certain."

"If your thoughts are about rendering judgment on what the other person is saying or doing, resist the temptation to speak," I was surprised to hear Cecile join the conversation. "Always wait until others are finished before responding and always affirm them first for sharing their ideas, even if you don't think it's a great idea at that moment. Do not impose your solutions. Ultimately, the role of the listener is to help the speaker come to a solution themselves. If you find yourself speaking more than anyone else in the room, there's a problem.

"Once, one of my managers approached me after a meeting. He helped me see that I had done almost all the speaking during the meeting, saying things like: *Do this, do this, do this, don't do that, and make sure you do this. And DEFINITELY - don't do that.* I was completely unaware of how I was leading until he pointed it out to me.

"You can always ask others: *Am I speaking too much? If I am, I give you permission to let me know.* If you are like me, and surely you are, you get excited about your ideas. That is fine! Passion creates movement, and you can maintain your enthusiasm, without oversharing.

"I received an email from someone who lived out the 'talk less and embrace silence' component of this and found it to work very well. Would you like to read it?"

"Sure. I'd love to!"

Cecile shared her screen, and this is what the message conveyed:

I had an experience with listening and the power of being heard this week that I had to share with you. We have a client who has a history of communication that, while well intended, is deeply rooted in pain and grief, and has a history of being received as harassing and aggressive in nature. To the extent where he had to be blocked from social media accounts and all communication with him had devolved into a bit of a contentious standoff. He was a newer manager and had begun contacting me. I could sense the underlying problem was he felt he wasn't being heard. You inspired me to take a different approach with him, and I decided to meet with him and asked another manager to join me as reinforcement. We met for nearly two hours and even though it was difficult in a few instances, we mostly simply listened ... and that's where the magic happened. His overall demeanor and energy changed, and he reached out to thank us for actually listening and hearing him. He attended and spoke at our bi-monthly client meeting last night. Every time he has spoken in the past, there has always been a very angry tone to his comments - until last night when he delivered remarks in a non-hostile way. Following the meeting, members of our admin team were shocked and approached me to ask what we did to help facilitate the change in his approach. My response? "We simply listened and allowed him to feel heard." Thank you for inspiring me to see a different way of approaching communication with him!

"Wow! What a powerful endorsement," I exclaimed. "*That's where the magic happened.* Great example! And I appreciated reading that the person who wrote to you made sure to use the Listening 2by2 method. I forgot to tell you that I have been using this approach too. I had a long conversation with Jaime. A real heart-to-heart. We cleared up a lot and I told her how I admired her leadership style. Then we discussed the Listening 2by2 approach to communication and agreed to be partners. We have been using this for the last month and it appears to be working.

"I really appreciate your sharing the email with me. That person simply listened. They didn't judge or condemn. He simply needed to be heard. I have to remember this story. I need to respond the way they did. I know I don't do it enough. Not even close. But since Jaime and I have started Listening 2by2, I feel like I have calmed down and, in many ways, even she has become more discerning and has improved her ability to ask probing questions."

"Ah, probing questions. That is part of ***E*** *– explain and ask questions*. We didn't intend to discuss this today, but I'm glad you brought it up," Vivian was glowing with pride. "Jeffrey, you are a leader and a manager because you are willing to lean into discomfort, you are willing to take a good hard look at yourself in the mirror, paying attention to those areas of management you do well and those areas in leadership that need some adjusting."

Cecile nodded and smiled. She looked at her watch. "We have gone over an hour, Vivian. Perhaps we should stop here?"

"Actually, I think I can continue. This has been invigorating and I'm not thinking about being sick. It's a pleasurable distraction from whatever I have. No offense, Jeffrey."

"None taken."

"Let's continue but first take a short break. I'd like to get some tea."

After the break, we discussed ***E*** *– Explain and Ask Questions*.

TALK LESS AND EMBRACE SILENCE

Don't hijack conversations

Don't jump in too fast

Ask before offering your thoughts

Hold back on judgments

Do not try to fix everything

Silence is revealing

"E"

EXPLAIN AND ASK QUESTIONS

Good listening is much more than

being silent while the other person speaks.

"I'm very intrigued by this next principle, ***E*** - *Explain and Ask Questions*. I'm searching for some clarity about it," I admitted. "If leaders are supposed to listen, how does explaining and asking questions come into play?"

"Fair enough," Cecile affirmed. "This is what we mean. Listeners shape conversations by asking questions that benefit the speaker, such as *Is there anything else you'd like to explain?* Good listening requires being thoughtful about what the speaker needs help with most and then crafting a question that would lead the speaker to search for an answer. Listeners need to ask questions to help someone delve deeper into their thoughts and experiences. This often brings to light new information and unexpected possibilities.

"Someone who really, truly listens, enables you to know when they are interested in you and what you're saying. They will draw you out by saying *Tell me more*. They ask questions that encourage thoughtful, deeper answers. Not merely *yes* or *no*. They probe. They are intentional. They help you to feel worthwhile. Like you matter. As though your life and your experiences are important."

I looked at Vivian sipping tea and wrapping her blanket tightly around her body. She was listening.

"Another method that is effective is *periodically* asking questions that promote discovery and insight. These questions can gently challenge old assumptions but do so in a constructive way. Sitting in silence and nodding does not provide sure evidence that a person is actually listening. Asking thoughtful questions tells the speaker the listener has not only heard what was said, but that they comprehend it well enough to know what might not have been said. They ask for additional information.

"Good listening is consistently a two-way dialogue, rather than a one-way interaction. The best conversations are active, drawing more and more out, to gain understanding and clarity. What we are accomplishing with our meetings with you is an example of explaining. Questions are important, but there comes a time when the listeners must answer and explain what they mean. This is where storytelling is helpful."

I listened and understood the need to explain. What I wanted more information about was how to ask probing questions.

"Here's a quick list of possible questions or responses (also a form of questioning) that may be helpful."

I always appreciate your ideas and think that's a great one. Would you explain a bit more about what you are thinking?

Tell me more about what happened the other day and let's see if we can find a solution together.

We know that the situation could have gone a bit more smoothly. What did we learn from the experience?

"The best listening includes interactions that build a person's self-esteem. Good listeners make the other person feel supported and conveys confidence. Issues and differences can be discussed openly and constructively. Relevant questions can help to explain and reveal more vital information. When a person feels heard and can share one's knowledge as fully as possible, self-esteem is reinforced. Effectiveness, productivity, and commitment are reinforced within the organization."

"My head hurts again," I said once Cecile paused. "I'm learning so much more than I expected to. I hope I can remember it all."

"Don't worry, Jeffrey. Asking good questions is perhaps the most difficult area to master of the LISTEN principles. Everyone needs improvement. You will see. Asking the right questions draws out the best in people. The key is trying to help others come to their own solutions without stepping in to fix the situation.

"As a leader, we must always remember that our way may not be the best way. It is a challenge to hold others accountable for what they commit to doing. We don't want to put those who work for and with us on the defense. Always use *we* statements instead of *I* statements. *How can we come up with a better solution to the problem? What did we learn from the experience?*

"Before we sign off, Jeffrey, Vivian and I have a challenge for you."

Surprised by this, I looked up from my notebook to see their faces on the monitor.

"Intentionally ask thoughtful questions of your family members. Around the dinner table is a safe place to start. Ask everyone to share their *high* and *low* moments from the day. Then ask follow-up questions similar to the ones we discussed today. We will start off next week's meeting discussing what you learned about yourself, what you felt about the process, and the reaction from your family. Think about if it became more natural and easier as the week progressed?"

"Sounds like a great idea!" Inside, my heart pounded so hard I thought it was visible through the screen. I was scared!

EXPLAIN AND ASK QUESTIONS

Ask questions that solicit more than “yes” and “no” responses

Ask questions to promote discovery and insight

Convey support of and confidence in others

Use “we” statements instead of “I” statements

Avoid putting others on the defensive

Use storytelling to clarify advice and answer questions

"N"
NEGOTIATE THE WIN/WIN

To become an expert at anything, we must practice, we must learn from our missteps, we must choose to do better next time.

With the changes the pandemic inflicted on businesses and homes, imposing an adjustment to day-to-day routines, it was another month before we could meet again. Thank goodness for technology. The tech companies were working overtime to help businesses be able to continue working and communicating. The day we met I was able to sit outside.

My company ensured all our employees had the bandwidth capable of supporting remote work from any location. At home, we improved our own capability. I didn't have to stay in what I affectionately referred to as my dungeon office. The sun was shining and warming my spirit. My pot of tea sat ready to be consumed and I anticipated a lively exchange with my listeners.

"So, what did you learn by listening to your family, umm, over the past month?," asked Vivian. She looked fantastic! I was thankful whatever she was battling a month ago was not the virus. Today, she wore a brightly colored shirt, and she smiled radiantly.

Cecile signed on just as we were getting started. She sat in her garden. I could see the flowers in bloom behind her. If I remembered correctly, she lived in a townhouse and had only a courtyard to care for in which she filled her spirit by planting an abundance of fragrant flowers.

Vivian lived in a renovated craftsman, not far from the city. She sat on her porch swing while balancing her laptop on her legs. Her home was simple, roomy, and a reflection of the farm she grew up on in the South. She told me once she couldn't imagine living in a flat or townhouse. She needed room to breathe.

After greeting both and thanking them for meeting with me, I started. "First of all, I learned that getting my girls to have simple conversation wasn't as easy as I thought it would be! In an age of technology, it's even more challenging to get them to open up. My wife and I had to be extra intentional about asking follow-up questions, so we didn't get the typical "yes" and "no" responses. We were so used to getting simple responses that we found it challenging to not accept them and turn to our own thoughts or a conversation between the two of us – excluding the girls completely.

"It took a lot of practice, and you were right. The more open-ended questions we asked, expressing genuine interest and desire to be in the know, the more our girls were willing to express themselves. To be honest, that may have been the most we heard from our eldest daughter in months! She noticed the change in me and thanked me for listening! By the end of the month, no one brought their phones to the dinner table. We were having conversations."

"Fabulous!," Cecile cheered. "That is so good to hear. I made the same effort over the past month and was reminded how much self-control is involved in being a good listener. Like any discipline, it takes a lot of effort, intention, and mental, emotional, physical, and spiritual strength to build strong bonds in relationships. I had a long day this past Wednesday, and I found myself wanting to doze through a conversation. But Jeffrey, it is in those moments that we need to be especially mindful of our desire to check-out and then to put in an extra effort to focus on the needs of others. The most important time to listen is when you'd rather not."

"That's the perfect segue to our final letter, ***N** – Negotiate the Win/Win*," Vivian interjected. "Listening never ends. Listening is an ongoing part of every successful relationship. The ultimate goal of listening is *to know others and to be known by others*. There is always more to learn about someone else. When we are intentional about listening, we keep learning and growing. It's about perspective. It's about empathy. It's about understanding another's point of view. It seeks a negotiation where both parties win. It's a Win/Win solution.

"A big part of leadership, as you know, isn't about always getting your way and the best deal. It's about working hard to reach a solution in which everyone walks away feeling heard, valued, and that they will benefit from the negotiated terms of an agreement. Most leaders don't do this very well. We don't think in terms of Win/Win because we often impose a Winner-Loser approach. Both are transactional in nature.

"The difference is, Win/Win seeks to find a common ground upon which to negotiate. Win-Lose is about the argument and coming out the victor. Those who enter a conversation from that position and don't get exactly what they want, stop negotiating. They stop listening."

Cecile continued. "Managers are often hired for their intellectual abilities but are fired for their lack of emotional abilities. Effective leaders understand that, in the end, corporations and businesses depend on people. They understand the necessity of interacting with those who work for and with them. Human-centric leadership skills, used daily, brings out the best in everyone. Human-centric leaders believe they can learn from others, no matter who they are or what position they hold in the organization."

"And they appreciate the heck out of people for the work they do and for their unique contributions. They always give credit where and when credit is due," Vivian added.

"Okay. Well, let me tell you a story that kind of fits in here," Jeffrey started. "I need to bring this up now because it not only speaks to this final principle, but also brings together the whole acronym for me. I've told you about Cesar and my interactions with him."

Vivian and Cecile nodded.

"Well, last week I had the opportunity to meet with him one-on-one. No Jaime. This was strictly social with a little bit of business. He was opening up a lot at work, thanks to our new approach, Listening 2by2. But there was something still wrong. He still scowled at me when I greeted him in the morning in my broken Spanish. His reaction was seen by everyone since, during this social distancing form of business management, our first meeting in the morning was now virtual and everyone attended. I even caught a glimpse of Jaime shaking her head one morning after I rendered my greeting in Spanish. I finally had to understand what the problem was and asked if he had some time after work to meet for a drink.

"That evening, we met virtually. I had a beer and he sat in his living room with a glass of water. He doesn't drink alcohol, he told me. We had small talk for a while and then I finally had to ask him why he had a negative reaction to my morning greeting.

"He explained that so many people make the mistake of assuming he is of Hispanic descent and, therefore, must speak Spanish. It turns out he is originally from New Mexico and is Native American. I was stunned and embarrassed. I couldn't believe I perpetuated my own assumptions for so long. It reminded me of Luca at the coffee shop and how I would have never thought she was studying to be a doctor because of how she looked.

"I realized that I never listened to Cesar. I never spoke with him. I never asked questions. I never got to know who he is. I just stuck with my version of Cesar and kept imposing it on him. Then something else happened."

I had to take a deep breath before I continued. I was about to reveal more about myself than I ever had in the past. I had to dig deep. Since my initial encounter with Jaime, I'd learned a lot about myself. I knew I was changing for the better. What was revealed next reinforced my transformation as a leader and a human being.

Vivian and Cecile sat silently waiting for me to compose myself and continue. It was in this silence that I realized its value.

I took a deep breath. "I heard a voice in the background. It was deeper than I thought it should be and had an endearing tone. Cesar looked toward the voice, smiled, and blew a kiss. He returned his attention to me and apologized. He told me his husband had just walked in from work.

"I'm positive he saw the shocked look on my face. I never, ever thought Cesar was gay. I am so embarrassed to tell you this. With one person, one single human being, I maintained my own version of who he is. In less than an hour, he taught me not to impose my definition of others on anyone but to take the time to talk, listen, and get to know them for who they really are and how they want to be known. It was humbling."

Again, there was silence. I stared at the screen and into the camera hoping one or both would tell me what happened was okay. Instead, they let the silence linger.

"Great leaders are compassionate; they show that they care," I heard Cecile say. "They have well-developed senses of humor and use it appropriately to diffuse tension and conflict. They use it to help make the work environment enjoyable and fun. They are sensitive to the relationships within the organization's culture, and they have and model respect for all person's values and beliefs. In addition, they allow others to define who they are for themselves.

"Impressive leaders are always paying attention. They are aware of what's going on around them. Above all, combined with all these characteristics, leaders constantly nurture their listening skills.

They are resolute about being intentional listeners. They understand that effective leadership begins with good listening and that the best relationships and results grow from there."

No reprimand for my story.

"Okay. Let me play devil's advocate," I responded. "What if people don't listen? What then? Everything you've shared with me these past months has been invaluable and it certainly has and will change the way I lead and manage. Yet, I know there are others who will resist."

"Jeffrey," Vivian's southern drawl slipped into place. "I'm impressed by you. You're asking all the right questions. The tension you are describing does happen, especially because listening isn't the sexiest subject to discuss and the least considered skill to develop. Cultivating a listening culture doesn't happen overnight. We need to keep working at it and tweaking things as we go. Listening has its roadblocks and I think it's important to discuss in greater detail some of those roadblocks.

"From our research and the school of hard knocks, we understand that managers who listen well are people leaders, and that's good for relationships and for business. People leaders tend to foster greater trust, openness, creativity, and job satisfaction among many other things.

"Yet, listening is counter-cultural. Our culture doesn't listen well. We don't need to get into politics, that's a whole other series of conversations we could have. But consider the way our leaders talk over and around one another. Our leaders aren't listening! They have an agenda, they have their worldviews, and they aren't willing to dig deep and examine how they have been approaching communication. Let's explore some of the roadblocks we have discovered over the years.

"First though, I need a fresh cup of tea. How about you?"

We all took a five-minute break to refill our drinks before Vivian continued.

"A few months ago, you may remember, I had you think of those people in your life who have been good listeners, including Jaime. You've done a good bit of reflecting on those who have essentially brought out the best in you. Now, I want you to do the same thing, but this time, I want you to think of those bosses, teachers, mentors, coaches, and of course managers, who weren't the best listeners. What made them that way? I'm going to time you. Ready. Set. Go!"

Vivian stopped her watch and then asked me to read my list.

1. Distracted whenever I was speaking.
2. Interrupted me before I was finished.
3. Didn't take my ideas seriously.
4. Always had the final say.
5. Never had time for me.
6. Everything felt transactional rather than relational.

I was curious. "Why is listening not more prevalent in the workplace? Why are most employees not listened to?"

"Jeffrey, I know we've very briefly discussed this during our successive meetings together. But let's dig into this even more to better understand," she turned to Cecile and nodded.

"Leaders can be afraid of losing a sense of power and authority over those they lead. Remember as you were transitioning and questioning your place and authority in the organization?"

Boy, did I remember.

"We fear being viewed as weak. We fear our leadership being questioned. We fear being perceived as indecisive. Those are all valid concerns."

"Yes they are," I chimed in.

Cecile smiled. "However, what we've found to actually be true is quite the opposite. Leaders and managers must make a trade-off between *gaining power* by bullying and intimidation or *gaining respect* by listening and being inclusive, showing that they value the people in the organization.

"You've heard the phrase *If the buck always stops with you, then you might feel the need to intimidate others to accomplish your goals*?"

I shook my head indicating I didn't know it.

"Okay, let me explain. Intimidation is often based on pressure and control. Respect, on the other hand, is based on humility, trust, delegation, and affirmation. Gaining trust by growing in respect is quieter, less controlled, less pressured. As always, all of it begins with listening."

I was finally beginning to understand how LISTEN is activated in the workplace and at home through intentional implementation.

"People ask me all the time, *Can you give me a list, maybe the 'top 10 things' I need to do to listen well?* Honestly, I bristle a bit when asked for a list. I know that people like lists. It helps to make remembering easier. I get it. But, as I have indicated already and will say again, *good and effective listening does not start and end with what you do. It starts and ends with what you believe*.

"We must believe that everyone is worthy of being listened to. We must believe that everyone has a story to tell. And we must believe that everyone has a need to be heard. When people feel heard, so much conflict is avoided, so much tension is diminished, and so much more is understood and clarified. It makes a significant difference."

"If I can interject. I have noticed a decline in conflicts and misunderstanding at work. I've noticed an increase in communication and collaboration. Even at home, we are talking *and* listening a lot more than we have in what feels like years."

"Yes!," Vivian raised her arms in victory. "So glad to hear that you are seeing change. Even small change is an improvement. All that being said, I do want to make this even easier to understand and remember. We believe that listening resembles a muscle. It requires training, persistence, effort, and most importantly, intention. It's estimated that we listen to others between a third to half of our lives. Listening well is extremely important. Intentional listening is vital."

One final question from Cecile. "What was the Win/Win that came out – no pun intended – of your conversation with Cesar?"

"I think we had a level of trust that didn't exist in the past. I learned to accept people for who they are, and Cesar didn't feel like he had to hide his home life anymore. Our relationship improved threefold and his commitment to our company was solidified."

"Perfect," Vivian and Cecile chimed in unison.

NEGOTIATE THE WIN/WIN

Listening is never done

The goal of listening is to know and be known

The desired result is a win-win solution

Listen from a place of humility

Listening is intentional

Listen for the *HOPE* that is unspoken

Reveal the "larger picture" of the situation or issue at hand

Be the Story Seeker

AFTERWORD FROM JEFFREY

To foster any relationship, both personally and professionally, and to achieve the best results, disagreements are unavoidable.

My listeners, Vivian and Cecile, continued meeting with me periodically over the next two years. We endured the pandemic and our businesses moved from survival to thriving. I remember telling them each time we met how implementing the LISTEN principles, incorporating Listening 2by2, and creating a listening culture has been transformational. On the home front, my relationship with my wife and children has dramatically shifted.

Jaime and I developed a professional bond that has grown stronger. She ultimately decided it was time to move in a new direction. We've had some delightful dinners together with our families and I've enjoyed hearing about her newfound success. Best of all, she has instituted Listening 2by2 and the LISTEN principles at her new workplace where she is the CEO. We've gotten to know each other as peers now and continue to collaborate.

When Jaime's father passed away, I was intentional about trying to give her my time and space to talk about her dad and how his passing affected her. I wanted her to know that I cared about what she was going through. I remember how lonely it felt when my dad died. Thinking that the workplace wasn't an appropriate space for processing those kinds of emotions and experiences, I rarely talked about what it was like, about what I felt. It's impossible to totally separate our personal lives from our professional lives. I now believe there can be healthy overlap.

I must tell you, some in the organization had a hard time trusting me at first and believing that my actions were sincere. They couldn't believe I didn't have hidden motivations or that I could change. Because of that, we lost some strong team members. But over time, those who stayed and those who joined our company began to realize that my level of care and concern for others was authentic. I became more encouraging, less driven, more present, less frantic, more productive, and less irritable.

I credit this change to Vivian and Cecile and their response when I asked them how they always seemed to have ample time for their family. Recall, our meetings were first thing in the morning. When we were finished they always left to be with their family. What they eventually shared was that they considered those with whom they work to be an extension of their home family. They brought to their workplace a family atmosphere. They always started their day moving from their respective families at home to their extended family at work. This was another way they built trust, incorporated listening, and reinforced core values.

I chose to follow their lead. In the beginning I was vulnerable. I was uncomfortable because Listening 2by2 was an alien concept to me. Yet, as we at work listened to each other with the mindset of our colleagues being part of our family, our relationships improved. I felt safer and was able to reveal more about myself. It made me more human and more approachable. The leadership team got to know me, and I grew as a leader.

I was able to open up to Jaime when we incorporated the Listening 2by2 leadership approach. In being able to share more about my doubts, challenges, and fears with Jaime, I began to verbalize them in meetings with other leaders. I believe they came to respect and understand me more, and I them. The organization became stronger.

As I mentioned above, this shift in leadership and management didn't suit everyone. We lost some of our employees, but the transformation and lessons learned from those who left helped us to refine our hiring process. We overhauled our notion of who we were looking for to ensure the people we hired were a good fit or could grow into the position and contribute to the success of the company. Melody was eventually promoted and has proven to be a valuable member of the team. And, yes, I did remember to talk to her about the marathon and even made time to support her the day she ran and finished the 26.2-mile challenge.

Cesar still serves as our comptroller, and I have stopped addressing him in broken Spanish. I've noticed that he smiles and laughs a lot more.

Luca, the barista at the coffee shop, graduated and was accepted to medical school. We have kept in touch, and I have taken on the role of mentor. She still has all her tattoos and piercings and the huge heart that will ensure she is an exceptional doctor.

I am a better person because my listeners modeled the value of the LISTEN principles and Listening 2by2 leadership method. They demonstrated what it means to listen and collaborate. Our organization is far stronger for it, too. The Listeners are wise, and I recommend their guidance to everyone who will, well… listen.

Until we listen again, the end.

FINAL THOUGHTS FROM VIVIAN AND CECILE

The best managers lead from a place of humility.

Like listening, humility is not thinking less of yourself;

it's thinking of yourself less.

So often, we've been told that being a good listener is like being a sponge that absorbs what the other person is saying. Most people think good listening comes down to doing three things: not talking when others are speaking, letting others know you're listening through facial expressions and verbal sounds (such as *mm-hmm*), and being able to repeat what others have said, practically word-for-word.

However, recent research suggests that these behaviors fall far short of describing good listening skills. Instead, good listeners are like trampolines. You can bounce ideas around with them. Instead of absorbing your ideas and energy, they amplify, energize, and clarify your thinking. They make you feel better not by passively absorbing what you are saying, but by actively supporting. This helps you gain energy and height, just like someone jumping on a trampoline.

Listening well does not prevent every misunderstanding, solve every problem, or alleviate tension. Relationships are never perfect. Communication is never free from misinterpretation. Ask yourself, *What do I do when people disagree with me?*

Now that you have been a part of our meetings with Jeffrey, we hope you realize that often we don't know how to answer that question directly. Often it is driven by the situation in which your leadership resides. Like Jeffrey's encounter with Jaime when she told Melody about the possibility of a promotion, using the LISTEN principles helped him frame and inform his approach prior to meeting with Jaime.

As we have been trying to emphasize, there are no cookie cutter answers, quick fixes, or one-size-fits all solutions. What we encourage is that you apply the LISTEN principles and keep asking those questions! Disagreements can be healthy and lead to even greater success if handled well. To achieve success, diverse perspectives will help you get there.

As a leader, your ideas matter. But remember, so do the ideas generated by your team members. The best managers who develop to be effective leaders learn not to function in a vacuum. There is a reason you, as a leader, have been handed the keys to the car. Your ability to work with people, within systems, organizations, and even families has been recognized and validated when given the responsibility to lead.

When others challenge or question your authority, your vision, or your passion, it's easy to become defensive, critical, and upended. In those moments, if trust has been established, and people believe you have their and the company's best interests in mind, these challenges can be addressed through listening and civil conversation.

If a member of your team, like Cesar, has an idea for how to achieve better results and the concept is diametrically opposed to your idea, take a deep breath, and listen. Weigh your options. Ask for others' opinions. Take a vote. But at the end of the day, trust yourself and your decision-making.

Listening helps to create contexts for productive conversations, positive interactions, and meaningful relationships. Listening is serving, metaphorically washing others' feet, putting their needs ahead of your own.

Remember, we can learn from everyone. Become a story seeker. Everyone has a story to share. Everyone is valuable and can contribute to the greatness of the whole of an organization. Make the time to LISTEN and value the contributions of those who work for and with you.

When we think we know it all, we will begin to fall. It has truly been our privilege to share Jeffrey's story with you.

Even though listening is a game-changer, we can't presume it will solve all our problems. As human beings, we aren't perfect.

Keep listening. *Simply listening.*

L.I.S.T.E.N.

L - LEAN IN and REMOVE BARRIERS

- **Eliminate distractions**
- **Look people in the eye**
- **Put technology away**
- **Encourage the introverts**
- **Remove barriers**

I - INTERESTED and CURIOUS

- **Be open to learning from everyone**
- **Invite others' ideas, visions, and dreams**
- **Acknowledge others' perspectives**
- **Ask probing questions**
- **Respond positively to others' input**

S - SIMPLIFY and SELF-CARE

- **Care for yourself**
- **Prioritize listening**
- **Delegate what others can do better than you**
- **Create intentional space to be fully engaged**

T - TALK LESS and EMBRACE SILENCE

- **Don't hijack conversations**
- **Don't jump in too fast**
- **Ask before offering your thoughts**
- **Hold back on judgments**
- **Do not try to fix everything**
- **Silence is revealing**

E - EXPLAIN and ASK QUESTIONS

- **Ask questions that solicit more than "yes" and "no" responses**
- **Ask questions to promote discovery and insight**
- **Convey support of and confidence in others**
- **Use "we" statements instead of "I" statements**
- **Avoid putting others on the defensive**
- **Use storytelling to clarify advice and answer questions**

N - NEGOTIATE the WIN/WIN

- **Listening is never done**
- **The goal of listening is to know and be known**
- **Listen from a place of humility**
- **Listening is intentional**
- **Listen for the *HOPE* that is unspoken**
- **Reveal the "larger picture" of the situation or issue at hand**
- **Be the Story Seeker**

The Story Seeker's Listening Checklist

☐ Have I been listening twice as much as I've been speaking? At home? At the office? In meetings? Anywhere else relationships can be developed?

☐ What have been the barriers to listening well? How can I remove some of those barriers?

☐ Have I noticed a change in my relationships? If yes, how might I foster even greater depth in those relationships? If not, why not?

☐ Is technology becoming too much of a distraction to listen well? Do I need to set boundaries with emailing, social media, or entertainment so I can be more fully present?

☐ Have I been asking good questions of those around me with the goal of knowing them more and better? Do I need to set aside time with someone in particular to hear more from them?

☐ The most important time to listen is when you'd rather not. When conversations are hard, do I double-down on listening to help me understand another's perspective, or do I double-down on being right?

☐ Am I making space to listen to myself?

ABOUT THE AUTHORS

Michael Gingerich and Tom Kaden envisioned an organization with the capability and capacity to be the ears and heart for those who need a compassionate person who listens. They are story seekers who created *Someone To Tell It To* for the storyteller. Through the years, a vault full of stories and success has been filled because of the leaders, team members, and volunteers who are compassionate listeners and meet as pairs with those who tell their stories, or as *Someone to Tell It To* calls them - *SOMEONES*. The listeners are always non-judgmental, trained to be fully present with the intent to not attempt to fix people, and have a belief that everyone has a story to tell and that everyone is *SOMEONE*.

Listening is when the magic happens.

Long-time friends who have a deep-seeded respect and love for each other, and an implicit trust, Michael and Tom are passionate about listening and have a vision and mission to bring compassionate listening to everyone's home, workplace, and relationship. Using their 2by2 Leadership™ model, they offer value to individuals and organizations seeking transformation and growth. In their homes, they practice intentionally being present with their families while balancing their mission to help storytellers.

Cultivating and fostering deep, authentic, and empathetic relationships drive their resolve to model listening as a genuine method to engage each person who enters their lives. Two of their influencers are Henri Nouwen and Fred (Mr.) Rogers. In the spirit of Mr. Rogers, they seek to create communities of acceptance, trust, appreciation, and encouragement.

Michael is a graduate of Lancaster Theological Seminary and Tom is a graduate of Asbury Theological Seminary. Their education is the foundation for their chosen mission to bring compassionate listening to businesses, nonprofits, individuals, and families.

Everyone has a voice, everyone matters, and we all need someone to tell it to.

Find out more about *Someone To Tell It To* at www.someonetotellitto.org and follow them on Twitter and Instagram: @some1totellitto and on Facebook at *Someone To Tell It To*.

ACKNOWLEDGEMENTS

Very early on in the process of writing this book, Michele Eby Chiarella, a dear friend and writing professional, encouraged, and affirmed us for this book as we were starting to compose it. Her experience and expertise helped to guide us as we formed the initial concepts and landed upon a story we had a vision to share.

Later, our *Someone To Tell It To* team member Kristin Sidorov McAleavey also encouraged and affirmed us as we made a final push to finish this book. Her professional writing and editing experience enabled us to begin to believe more strongly that we had something of value to put out into the world.

We thank the Beta Readers who took the time to read the manuscript and who gave such encouraging and thoughtful responses to it - Joshua Bonn, Todd Cox, Angie Dickinson, Rob Harman, Donna Hunter, Anthony Johnson, Janet Olkowski, Paul Sokolofsky, and Michael Yang. Your comments confirmed and reassured us that the message, direction, and tone of the book were relatable and appropriate. Your suggestions and questions enabled us to address concepts that brought greater clarity and focus to the message. You helped us to believe that we had a book worth publishing, a concept worth sharing, and a voice worth hearing.

We thank Jon Gordon and Shola Richards who endorsed our book and shared their voices in resonance with the listening movement this book supports. They are men who understand the power of listening deeply and well.

They believe that lives and cultures will be changed when we focus on one another with respect, intentionality, and positivity, offering a safe presence to get to the essence of what needs to be said.

We thank Ken Blanchard, who took our phone calls whenever we reached out, invited us into his home a continent away to get to know us and our mission better. He assured us that we were on to something transformational with *Someone To Tell It To*. Over the years since we first met, he has remained an inspiration and a source of light as we grew and activated our mission in a way that modeled compassion, integrity, and generosity of spirit - just as he has done in his life and career.

We thank Stephanie Shirley, whose public relations expertise is taking us to places we could not have imagined as we publish this book. Her understanding of what we need to do to promote the book, to influence the cultures of organizations, and to strengthen personal relationships, is helping us to create change that is deeply needed.

And to Isabelle Harman, our editor - and so much more - thank you for believing in us. You told us that we deserve to be authors. You told us that there is great value to what we are doing and offering. You pushed us to believe in and own our message, to embrace that we have become listening experts. You helped this story to be polished and deepened, to be more engaging and descriptive, to be able to resonate with audiences who have not previously known our work.

Your organizational wisdom, leadership expertise, and genuine desire to help ease the suffering of others has inspired us since day one. We can't wait to write many more books together! And thank you for listening to us, receiving good ideas, not so good ideas, and everything in between with understanding, a willingness to learn, and a deep desire to help us reach our goals. You got us over the finish line. Writing a book is much like running a marathon. It's a long, meandering, often lonely, sometimes frustrating, occasionally painful slog. When we didn't quite know how to get to the finish line, you showed us - and accompanied us on - the way.

MORE BY TOM KADEN AND MICHAEL GINGERICH

Someone To Tell It To: Sharing Life's Journey

Someone To Tell It To: Moved with Compassion

BY TOM KADEN

CHAPTERS IN *CHICKEN SOUP FOR THE SOUL*

Chicken Soup for the Soul: The Power of Positive (2012)

- "Uncovered"

Chicken Soup for the Soul: Angels Among Us (2013)

- "Stranded"

Chicken Soup for the Soul: A Book of Christmas Miracles (2017)

- "Stranded"

BY MICHAEL GINGERICH

A Light Shines in the Darkness

CHAPTERS IN *CHICKEN SOUP FOR THE SOUL*

Chicken Soup for the Soul: The Cancer Book (2009)

- "Fear"

Chicken Soup for the Soul: Find your Happiness (2011)

- "The Returning Light"

Chicken Soup for the Soul: Family Caregivers (2012)

- "A Wonderful World?"

Chicken Soup for the Soul: Raising Kids on the Spectrum (2013)

- "Obsession"

CPSIA information can be obtained
at www.ICGtesting.com
Printed in the USA
BVHW050750040322
629847BV00022B/56